Textual Intercourse

DATING AND RELATING
IN A CELLULAR WORLD

Laura Saba

RUNNING PRESS
PHILADELPHIA · LONDON

9   8   7   6   5   4   3   2   1
Digit on the right indicates the number of this printing

Library of Congress Control Number: 2008931540

ISBN 978-0-7624-3642-2

Book design by Amanda Richmond
Edited by Jordana Tusman
Typography: Berkeley Book, Metallophile, Coquette & Wendy

Running Press Book Publishers
2300 Chestnut Street
Philadelphia, PA 19103-4371

Visit us on the web!
www.runningpress.com

for James Bach—

OURS IS THE LOVE
THAT TEXT BUILT

Introduction

Textual Pain and Pleasure

AS IF ROMANTIC RELATIONSHIPS were not difficult enough—now modern technology has opened the door to even more misunderstandings, misinterpretations, and miscommunications. The elimination of inflection and expression, and the rapid-fire pace at which text messages occur, not to mention the temptation to read a text through the rose-colored glasses of love's great hope, frequently leaves women with a desire for greater communication and deeper levels of connectedness.

Women and men have bravely entered this new communications frontier birthed by e-mail, as willing explorers of the terrain that evolved into instant messaging, and finally into the "communicate anywhere" land of cell phone texting. No more waiting at home for the phone to ring. Even if you're in a meeting or out with the girls, you can still send or receive text anywhere.

Perhaps you yourself are among the ever-increasing numbers

who have begun or ended a relationship via text. Or you've texted a guy when feeling insecure, just to make sure he didn't forget you exist. Or perhaps you confessed you weren't that into him, while safely protected by that tiny screen. Nothing beats being able to do your dirty work without the mess.

But have you ever had cause to take a few pixel pauses as you wondered—should you really have hit the *send* button? Or maybe you've waited with bated breath for that satisfying vibration heralding a return message from your love only to find it didn't come when expected. Did you immediately text your friends to analyze why he didn't text back? Did you panic, wondering if you had somehow failed to stimulate his textual pleasure with what you thought were textual witticisms?

Ah yes, instant access in both directions, and with it a wide array of pros and cons as you discover you have all the more ways to experience exhilaration or rejection. As if there hadn't been enough before. Indeed, modern gals receive dozens of little messages a day to run past their friends for interpretation. Precise analyses of messages, emoticons, and even pacing are heard in the office, on the subway, over cocktails, even in restaurant restrooms.

With this new frontier come new challenges: When should you talk in person as opposed to texting? How much text is too much? What does it mean if he doesn't text back immediately? What is okay to text and what should you say in person?

Do you read a text when out on a date? What about when in a meeting?

The questions and potential faux pas seem endless. As with any new frontier, the territory of instantaneous textual communication is largely uncharted. It may look and feel safe, but until it is fully explored, one never can know what challenges are lurking around the next virtual bend on the information highway.

Along with all the associated pleasures of text can come a great deal of pain, not only that of repetitive stress injury from all that texting, but the sudden panic that accompanies self-doubt. Did you ever think a cute little phone could cause your confidence to fly away faster than a message on a T3 connection?

Well, you are not alone. All of us are in the same boat. It was bad enough when we had to try to decode men and their cryptic words, actions, and inactions the old-fashioned way. But now, thanks to modern technology, along with the wonders of instant communication come the pains of more text to decode and the speed of return text to be analyzed. What did that abbreviation mean? You're cut—or you're cute? Is he breaking up with you or thinking you're adorable? There are additional worries. How could you suggest he was out with someone else when he clearly demonstrated he was thinking of you? He sent you a text!

As much as this new and highly textual age has been a hit

with women, it has also contained those old demons: *mis*communication, *mis*interpretation, and *mis*understanding. What is a girl to do?

Don't get your pixels in a bunch! You have in front of you a guidebook to romantic territory girls a generation ago would've never imagined, but one that today gives us daily cause for concern. Never again will you feel insecure during that ongoing exchange with your partner via text, otherwise known as "textual intercourse." This book will help you avoid textual impotence by walking you through the rules of text-iquette; textual interpretation and pacing; abbreviation navigation; maintaining textual boundaries; and red hot text. You'll learn how to use text to enhance your relationship and help you avoid the pitfalls of textual communication, while helping you stay safe both emotionally and physically through textual prophylactics you can use as you dive into this wide new world of textual exploration. This book is your answer.

SOME PLEASURES *of*
INSTANT TEXTUAL COMMUNICATION

* No matter where you go, you can count on enjoying that vibration which announces the fact that you are wanted. In fact, not only are you aware of it, so is everyone else around you.

* You can savor the look of disappointment on the faces around you when they realize it wasn't their phone announcing textual attention.

* You are always in the loop, always the one with the latest, greatest information.

* You get to communicate a lot of information without wasting time on the phone.

* You get to deliver uncomfortable information without having to deal with the emotional response on the other side.

* You are never truly alone.

Chapter 1

The Art of
Textual Attraction

ANYONE WITH ACCESS TO A CELL PHONE can send text messages (TMs). However, there are regular old text messages, and then there are unforgettable TMs, the kind that pique interest, the kind that echo through one's mind all day long—the kind that help turn a relationship from good to great. If you want your fingers to be stroking unforgettable text, don't worry— you can do it. This book will walk you through the art and craft of the world's greatest textual techniques.

What makes great text? There are many different elements that contribute. One element of great text is the way it is received, and that part can be really tricky. How can you control how someone interprets your message? The reality is that you can't; however, you can make good decisions when creating text, especially by considering the content, intent, and time sent. The timing and circumstance of how a text is received can play a tremendous role in that interpretation. While you can't look into a crystal ball to see if this is a good time to send a TM or not, you can use some forethought.

Memorable text also needs to be crafted so it is as easy as possible for the recipient to really *get* what you mean. Remember, TMs are devoid of many of the factors that enrich in-person communication, such as voice inflection, tonality, and body language. While that is lost in other forms of written communication, such as a love letter or e-mail, the text message loses so much more. How much information can you really fit into such a limited number of characters?

The answer to that question can depend on a lot of things. While it's true you have only a limited number of characters to work with, if you are clear as to what message you hope to deliver via text (and we all know it is often supposed to *mean* so much more than what it says!) and establish a good baseline communication, master the art of brevity, learn to use clear abbreviations, utilize emoticons, and ensure that you deliver both message *and* intent in those few characters, a tiny message can pack a big punch. It isn't as complicated as it sounds, I promise. And it is worth taking the time to learn these techniques, because mastering communication in any form empowers you. If you master this short, direct form of communication, you will get far more out of textual communications, and your relationship overall. Carefully crafted TMs can affect how someone perceives you and your relationship. And finally, a text message, good or bad, can change the course of someone's day entirely.

Doubt it's possible? Do you deny that Carrie Underwood's day probably took a surprising turn when she was famously dumped via text message? Now there's a TM that could really change your day! Imagine the tingle of excitement at the vibration of your cell heralding a new message from the one you love, only to open it up and find out that you've been dropped!

Think that's bad? A friend of mine was notified of the death of a loved one via text. Again, wow. However, bad news isn't the only way in which a TM can turn your day around. I was notified of the approval of a big work contract via TM. And I never saw my friend Jen as happy as she was when she received notification that "the money has been transferred to your account" via TM.

Those, however, are the more obvious ways in which a TM can affect your life. What, though, of the well-timed, brilliantly crafted message that interrupts a rotten workday to remind us that our life is bigger than what is in front of us right now, and that we are loved, appreciated, and cared for? What, too, of the message that inspires or titillates during the course of a difficult or otherwise boring afternoon? The right message from the right person can galvanize us into action and can inspire us to create an amazing day for ourselves, no matter how difficult it has been thus far. In fact, if you take the time to assess who and what you want to bring to your life and the lives of others when TMing, you can have a dramatic effect on those you interact with and in the process, on the quality of your own life.

So get ready to take a walk through the empowering process of mastering the art of great text.

▃▃▊▊ Textual Preference

BEFORE YOU EXPLORE the nuts and bolts of your everyday text life, you may want to take a moment to look at your textual preferences. If you're like most people, you didn't necessarily realize you had any; rather, you just saw texting as something you do throughout the course of a day, almost on a whim. Right there you discover a key factor in the process of turning everyday text messaging into a powerful tool that can raise TM to an art form—a highly seductive art form that can help you get the things you want in life.

A good place to start is by asking yourself the "why" of your textual interactions. Why are you bothering to communicate? What do you hope to achieve? We all have motives that define our preferences, even if we aren't consciously aware of them.

Once you learn to recognize them, you will be able to look at ways in which to deliver great text to move you toward satisfying your greatest goals, while enabling you to express your most amazing self in the process. So, let's begin to take a look at your textual mindset.

Do you see TM as simply a means to dash off some information? C'mon, you just *have* to share every passing moment of the day with your guy, don't you? I mean, if it keeps you connected, it just has to be good, right? And hey, you can't help thinking about how cute or sweet he is, or how much you love him, or how happy you are when you're together, or thinking about him, or talking about him. You'd better text him every time those thoughts pop into your head, 'cause you'd want him to do the same, right? If that is you, your textual style is *all thoughts all the time*. You just can't help sharing every last thought that flies through your brain with him, even if you've told him the same thing a million times before. You assure yourself it is *just to let him know*, even if you could've shared the same information or emotions with him when you see him again. Besides, you can never say "I love you" too much, right?

What about when you're just a bit insecure? If you're feeling a little unpretty, or those trust issues are flaring again, it's time to reach for the trusty cell phone and get some reassuring textual attention to make you feel better, dontcha think? If this is you, your textual style is *validate me, please...?!* Your real reason for texting banal content is to get feedback, or rather, attention, a response that tells you someone cares and that you are okay.

Perhaps you've even gone so far as surrendering to your baser desires, sending messages designed to incite, a sneak attack when he can't fight back. I mean, it was how you were feeling, so it was within your rights to send those messages, right? Hey, if he didn't want texts like that he should (or shouldn't have) ____. And he's supposed to love you; he should want to hear every little thought going through your mind even when he's angry, even if he isn't in a position to respond at the moment. If that is you, you're a *sucker punch* kind of texter, taking advantage of someone's inability to strike back, and perhaps hiding behind the safety of a tiny screen rather than face his direct response.

Or maybe you're shaking your head. You don't text for any of *those* reasons. You simply text 'cause it's fun, you want to share your day with him, or you miss him. Nothing wrong with that. That makes you a *freestyle texter*. Nothing necessarily wrong with your text life, but it also may not be something great, either. It is kind of like the difference of looking at life from a "why not?" perspective as opposed to a "why?" When you ask "why not?" you only look at what could go wrong if you do it. If you ask "why?" you are looking at what great things can enter your life if you do. And if you begin to look at the "why?" of your text life, you will be in a position to create incredible textual intercourse.

So, do you send off a TM based on any or all the needs we described above, you know, from that "why not?" kind of perspective? You can argue that your reasons for texting are justified in your mind, every single time, right? Probably some or even most of your girlfriends would even support those reasons for texting—they support your many phone calls, don't they? Remember, though, if you keep doing something the same way you always have, you are going to get the same results. For ages girls have been quick to express themselves without taking a moment to pause, to step back and look at the big picture. But what if you took a moment to take a deep breath and ask yourself how it looks and feels on the receiving end?

Sure, your reasons for wanting to text are valid for you, so you set his pocket vibrating. However, even if you feel justified in sending your message, have you thought of the impact the timing and delivery of the message will have?

Before you get all hot-fingered, perhaps you *should* take a moment to ask yourself, who does *he* see when he reads that message? Does he see the justification that I see? Am I coming across as his *it girl* or as *that girl*? Does he "get it," or is he creating his own interpretation of what I mean? You know how you call your girlfriends to try to figure out what he means about things? Guess what? He does the same thing. Do you want to be leaving yourself open for less than amazing feedback?

Think about this: Your texts that were intended to let him

know he's on your mind and loved, if paced wrong, or sent without clarity and discretion, could, instead of letting him know he's in a healthy, supportive relationship, give off the feeling that he's dating an insecure, obsessive *that girl* who forever has to keep track of him. Or worse yet, he may feel textually assaulted. Remember, the male mind doesn't always perceive things the same way the female mind does.

Additionally, your messages regularly updating him on your life throughout the day could come across as "wow, we are so connected" or "this girl can't do anything for herself; it's like she needs my approval to do anything. Is she going to text me when she needs to use the bathroom?" And speaking of which, *please* don't be one of those women we hear playing with her cell phone buttons in the public stalls! There's a time and a place for everything! Do you really want to bring him with you into *every* area of your life?

The time and attention you give to examining the bigger goals of your TMs can play a huge role in how he views you and your relationship. So before you send off text that could be interpreted as panicked, neurotic, obsessive, or pushy, stop and consider whether you should be fingering your keypad at all, much less hitting *send*. The time for thinking about who you want to be textually, and how you want to come across in textual interactions, is now, at a neutral moment, not when you're in the throes of textual intercourse. Here are some questions to help you determine your automatic, unconsidered textual preferences and the ones that you can choose to create instead.

CREATING YOUR TEXTUAL IDENTITY

* Do you want to come across as independent, or as needing his input in all that you do?

* Do you want to be recognized as someone who has an exciting, fulfilling life, or as a girl who needs a man to make it exciting for her?

* Do you want to seem together or neurotic?

* Do you want to create an atmosphere where you just can't wait to connect again, or a suffocating atmosphere where each party feels obligated to check in?

* Do you want to come across as caring or as a stalker?

Too often failure to think about our actions can give others an impression quite different from that which we actually feel, believe, or are.

Recognize, too, that the difference between a clingy, obsessive, or neurotic gal and an emotionally healthy one isn't necessarily that one is more emotional than the other. It is that one allows those emotions to run her life. The last thing you want to do is suppress your feelings and emotions; that has been shown to contribute to unhappiness, high levels of stress, and even illness. No, what I'm asking you to do is get honest with yourself about your emotions, then ask yourself if the ways you are choosing to express them really reflect who you are and who you want to be. You can't control feelings themselves, and there are no right or wrong feelings, but you do have control over what you do with them and how you put them on others.

If you are feeling jealous, insecure, or unloved, acknowledge those feelings. We all have moments when we feel like that. And you know what? It's okay; it shows you're—gasp—human. Recognize the emotions and say hello to them. However, ask yourself if you send an obsessive stream of TMs, or demand attention in the midst of his workday, simply because you have trust issues and need reassurance. Is that going to help you reach your goal of feeling loved and secure in your relationship in the big picture? Or is it more likely to achieve just the opposite, possibly even driving him away, or at the very least, making him less likely to offer up reassurance on his own? Just because you are experiencing certain emotions doesn't mean you have to act upon them.

If what you crave is assurances, let him know that at a neutral time, not when you are in the heat of an anxiety attack. First, though, ask yourself what *would* make you feel safe and secure. Then tell him directly what you need to feel secure, if it is reasonable. If your answer to that is, "for him to be available at my every whim," recognize that while he may be able to do that some of the time, you are perhaps asking something a bit unreasonable. When he's at work, or playing third base in the big game, is it really fair to demand he respond to an irrationally driven TM simply because you need assurance at that moment?

Instead, remind yourself that you are indeed lovable and all the more so because you are becoming more and more aware of the demands your TM may place on the recipient. Then turn your attention to activities that make you the *wonderful you* that you are! Spend some time with your friends; work out; get outdoors; volunteer; get creative and write, or draw, or make music; learn to cook a fantastic new dish; take up a new sport; learn a new language; develop a new hobby; plan a trip with the girls; do something to make *you* even *more wonderfully you*, and give yourself a pat on the back for trusting in your greatness and finding new ways of developing your persona, as opposed to seeking validation from someone else.

Many people go through life thinking only about their

immediate needs and concerns. They pick up a phone, and send off an e-mail or TM that is driven by their need in the moment without considering how it affects their relationships in the big picture, or even whether reaching out habitually is truly helping them. Too many times we behave this way solely out of habit. Don't get me wrong: if you've a true emergency, by all means, reach out! Just make sure it really is one, rather than habit, or worse yet, boredom.

If you take the extra time to think about where and when the recipient is when receiving your text, and if it is well received and is moving you in the direction you want to go, you will find that you are developing a whole new quality in your textual life, and your relationship overall. Now stop and think about something else. Every moment you waste sending off needy, clingy, or boredom-inspired TMs *just because,* is a moment stolen from building a more incredible life for incredible you! Think of all that wasted potential. You could be developing a new talent, exploring a new hobby, advancing in your career, and letting your guy see what a healthy, fascinating gal you are.

I want to make something clear: I am NOT suggesting you alter your personality, lie, or play games; in fact, I hope you never even consider those as options. I'm saying nail down your true identity; ask yourself questions to determine who you are, what actions and behaviors reflect that, which detract from it, and what ways your time is best spent toward helping create a wonderful life for you, and a wonderful relationship with that special guy. Again, I'm not asking you to ignore your emotions; I'm asking you to question your current textual preferences, to examine things like whether *this moment* and *this method* is the best way to express your feelings, needs, and desires successfully, and whether it is contributing to your life and relationship alike.

Next time you are feeling needy, and we all do at some time or other, ask yourself if this is the time to express that to him, or if it is better saved for when you are truly in crisis. If you feel you must reach out now, consider how you are going to reach out. What is your goal? Just to hear a response? To get an "I love you"? If so, send messages that demonstrate your most lovable self, not a clingy, desperate self.

The same holds true regardless of what your textual style is. If you're a *sucker punch* texter, ask yourself, is that who you really want to be? Or do you want to develop yourself into a dynamite textual creature? The choice is yours. You can either waste your time and dilute your relationships with banal, needy, clingy, annoying textual activities, or you can explore ways in which to become a confident, exciting, witty textual temptress.

Who do you want to be? Who is the best you, at the core of your being? The answers to those questions will help determine your future textual preferences. Once you decide for yourself that you want to be a textual goddess in full control of her life and relations, you will learn that it is far more fulfilling to create gorgeous textual intercourse that permeates your relationship on every level imaginable than to waste your time with unfulfilling, empty text.

Why don't you take the time to define for yourself some answers to the questions below:

Who do you want to be in your relationship?

What are your textual preferences?

How would that person behave when interacting with someone else via text message?

⬛ Textual Confidence

Once you've determined your textual preference, you will want to proceed in a way that demonstrates that you are, indeed, a fully self-actualized woman who is in control of her life and her emotions, rather than being run ragged by them. This appears to others as confidence. Confidence is sexy. Develop confidence in your textual performance and you completely change the atmosphere of your communications and the responses they elicit. What does confident textual intercourse feel like? It comes across as clever, teasing, and tempting, never as clingy or "overtexted." It isn't so much in the words you use as the ways in which you use them, and the motives behind them.

What is the secret to developing that perfect balance inherent in confident communication? A good sense of self, again, knowing who and how you want to be interacting, and knowing the rules and language of the "game" of TM.

Now that you've thought a bit about how you want to express yourself during textual intercourse and begun to consider the outcome you hope to generate with your textual indulgences, how do you become textually confident? It is simple. You learn the ins and outs (pun quite intended) of the textual world. Once you have a firm grip on your sense of self, of who you want to be in your communications, and how to create an exchange that reflects who you genuinely are, the goals of your specific interaction will become clear.

That is the first part. It is then simply a matter of massaging the other elements into place, and a large part of that is education. Learn to pay attention to rhythm and pace. Remember, men typically like it fast and to the point, so develop an intimate understanding of the use of language and the response it can incite; learn the keypad so you can use your fingers fast and accurately; increase your textual vocabulary for clear, fast communication; know the rules of the game and how to respect the boundaries of others, and how to set textual boundaries for yourself; and know and practice safe text. Do this, and you will be free to have fun with it, to be playful or teasing; if and when you are ready to get serious, you'll know how to make sure your textual partner is ready for it, ensuring everyone is fulfilled by your textual intercourse.

If you cover those basic elements, which sound like a lot but can be learned rather quickly, you will become a master of textual intercourse, and with that mastery comes that gorgeously sexy textual confidence.

▁▃▅█ Textual Attention

ONCE YOU'VE DETERMINED what aspect of yourself you wish to share during textual communication, and developed your textual confidence, you will be in a position to command some serious textual attention.

Why should you even worry about commanding his textual attention? If you're asking this, I ask you in return: Why would you reject the opportunity to have instant access to your man at any moment of the day? Mastering the ability to command positive textual attention creates an even more exciting, more deeply connected relationship. Our ability to use language to shape and mold our experiences allows us to take our lives and our relationships to an entirely different height. When you learn the art of textual communication you will discover it empowers you not only to keep in touch, but to keep your romance going strong, helping you avoid common stressors such as miscommunication, confused expectations, and distance. And it can even bring a whole new level of fun into your life. It is also a way to keep yourself in the forefront of his mind—never a bad thing if done right.

The key is learning to do all of this in a positive way. Just as with everything else in life, you can command textual attention in a positive or negative way. In the same way a child will act out to gain negative attention if feeling neglected, some people inadvertently use TM to command negative attention, feeling that *any* attention and *quantity* of attention are more important than the inconsequence they may feel otherwise. That won't happen to you, though. You hold a key to empowered text in your hands. You will quickly realize that *quality* textual attention is far superior to the negative, in fact so much so that you'd never consider accepting anything less. You must have a sense of this, because you put your magic cell down long enough to pick up this book.

Avoiding Textually Transmitted Diseases

Unfortunately, with the advent in popularity of text messaging, there are those looking to kill all the fun, so before you jump into text, get educated about textually transmitted diseases so you can dive into a world of textual exploration without worrying about catching something. Remember, prevention is the best key to good textual health.

What is a cell phone virus? Hackers have learned to send a virus to our "smart phones." They are delivered as fake ringtones, spyware, or even games. Know the signs and symptoms:

- Is your phone working slowly?
- Is it getting a lot of spam messages?
- Is it crashing?

Any or all of those symptoms could indicate a virus. You also want to watch out for phishing, when someone is trying to trick you into giving out personal information that could leave you at risk for identity theft. To help keep yourself safe, try the following prophylactics:

- You can use an antivirus program, just as you do for your computer. Check out Symantec, or any of the others that are springing up. The program downloads right to your cell phone. This will both scan for and remove viruses, as well as preventing unauthorized access.
- Make sure to "lock" your cell phone (directions come with your phone) and don't give your password out.
- Be wary of "free" downloads of games or ringtones! Don't accept e-mail from those you don't recognize.
- If you use Bluetooth, keep it off when not in use; hackers can pick up the signal and transmit viruses.

So, how does one go about commanding positive textual attention? As with other forms of communication, there are many ways to grab his attention. Some may think the key to this is direct, graphic content. While that will certainly work at times, true seduction begins with the mind, and if you master the art of commanding textual attention you will understand that there are many nuances to this skill. For instance, if you learn to stimulate his mind without using strictly naughty text, you will raise the bar on your relationship. You can tease; you can drop him a tempting message or a tasty tidbit of information that you know he will appreciate; you can remind him of something important; or you can send a quick pick-me-up. The idea is to deliver short, exciting bursts of information that hint at how much more there is, and what a multifaceted gem you are, without giving away the whole enchilada. You want to leave him eager to see or speak with you again. If you give it all away in text, what will there be to talk about or titillate him with when you are together again?

Rather, text should be like an appetizer, just a bit of a reminder that you are someone mentally, emotionally, and physically stimulating who makes his life better in every way. It is not therapy, nor should it be used simply to alleviate boredom, with the exception of an occasional indulgence. If you do so indulge, I recommend that you be the one to end the TM session first. After all, you have an exciting life to get back to, don't you? The more exciting he envisions your world when you are away from him, the more he will be champing at the bit to get your attention again. Men enjoy challenges; let him enjoy having to earn your attention a little bit here and there, especially in your text life.

Now that you see there are reasons to command his textual attention through your confident utilization of TM, and that it can indeed be done, this book will show you how.

Chapter 2

Textual Enhancement

IF YOU'RE HOLDING THIS BOOK you probably already realize that your cell phone has the potential to significantly enhance not only your text life, but also your sex life, and your love life overall.

The ability to keep in touch with your partner—to flirt, tease, and tempt him all day long, building up to the thrill of the moment when you are reunited after a long day apart—can be priceless. So can the ability to step in and share with him your other assets, demonstrating the overall support dynamo you can be. Empower yourself by understanding how these things can work to your advantage, and you'll grow to see even more clearly why it is important to pause and think before hitting the *send* button. Once again, ask yourself, if it isn't enhancing your relationship, why are you doing it, rather than something that does? And remember, any TM can be turned into one that improves your relationship, if you focus on textual intention.

Know, too, that besides all that great flirting, there are many other ways in which your cell phone and TMs in general can raise the bar in ways that allow you to greatly enhance your relationship—and this chapter will show you how.

▪▪▊▊ Good Vibrations

WHEN YOU CREATE A HEALTHY TEXT LIFE, your relationship can be greatly enhanced by the added tingle of excitement good vibrations throughout the day can bring. Just knowing you are thinking about each other can boost your mood, casting a glow across your day that is far brighter than the one on your cell phone screen. This is the first way, of course, in which TMs can be used to improve your relationship.

You already know, I'm sure, the ways that little vibration heralding a new communication can make someone feel. Imagine how much better that can be once you take time to examine content and timing before sending it.

Everyone likes to be thought of, and thought of well! Contacting your love interest throughout the day just to pass along the tingle of excitement that lets him know he's wanted can be fantastic, so long as you don't cross that line into obsession. If you're behaving like his *it girl*, then you've found the right balance that says, "Oh yeah, she's into me," rather than, "Oh no, it's her again!"

So how do you create that balance? You connect with him throughout the day in ways that are legitimate, such as filling him in on a breaking piece of information you know he is particularly interested in, or giving him a quick, playful hello that hints at a tease, and then get back to your day; don't engage in ongoing texting. Let him regard your text messages as treasured delights, rays of sunshine cast across his day, rather than something he can come to take for granted. Think about it. Don't you want him eagerly reaching to see if it is indeed a message from you, rather than telling his friends he's not even going to check it now?

TEN GREAT REASONS TO TEXT HIM

1. To congratulate him on how his team just made the playoffs/won the series.

2. To tell him you tried his suggestion, and it worked GREAT (but only if you did).

3. To warn him that his (boss, mother, professor, etc.) is on the way up.

4. To allude to the great time you're going to have later in the evening.

5. To express how great last night was (but don't go overboard, and only if you've been seeing him for a while). Don't do this after the first time you've been intimate.

6. To ask him to pick up something for tonight (only sexy/fun stuff like condoms, beer, wine, etc.). If you start using TM as a things-to-do list, you will earn the reputation as a textual nag and his friends will tease him for being so text-pecked.

7. To tell him he was right about _____, and you're so lucky to have such a smart guy in your life! (Only if it's true!)

8. To provide an escape from a meeting you know he doesn't want to be at.

9. To ask his advice on something crucial that you know he considers himself an expert on (but only if you intend to seriously consider his advice).

10. To apologize when you've erred (though again, best left for in person, but if you can't do that, this is the next best thing).

What are some good reasons you can think of as reasonable and supportive for texting him in an unobsessive way?

Remember, you don't want to use all ten reasons in the same day. Pacing! Timing! Don't inundate him! Pick one and choose it well, and operate with sincerity or it will backfire. It would be awesome, too, if you could combine several of them into one message, such as: U were right, my boss sed yes! Lookin 4ward 2 repeat of last nite. Can't wait to try that wine u r bringin!

Too, you're not his secretary, or his keeper; you're not setting out to flatter him. This is not about subjugating yourself or stroking his ego; it is a matter of recognizing that these are things we all like to hear, or areas in which we can all use a little support. If it is authentic, takes little effort on your part, and makes someone feel great, is that subjugating yourself? Of course not! We all like to hear occasionally that we were right on about something, or that we helped someone out, and we certainly all like to know someone is watching out for us, on our side when we walk into that meeting from hell, or when we are facing a complicated event. This isn't about playing games, this is about taking time to pause and ask, what would really make his day? If you don't know where to start with that, try thinking of what would make *your* day; but don't assume the answers are the same for him. Use your own ideas as a springboard, and then try to imagine how he would respond to such.

Contemplate his interests. Think about things he's shared and the kinds of things he lights up over. Those are likely the things that make him feel good. And then, if you are feeling moved to make his day, send him the gift of good vibrations. If you are selective in your TM habits, and spend a moment focusing on textual intent, you will hold in your hands the power to cast powerfully great vibrations across his day!

...il Is It Good for You Too?

COMMUNICATION IS KEY TO A GOOD RELATIONSHIP. Nothing can be more frustrating than a guy who constantly runs late; it can leave the other party feeling quite unsettled, not to mention taken for granted or unappreciated. Thanks to the convenience of cellular technology, you can remain in close textual contact, even when life interferes with your plans. You can check with each other to ensure an unplanned change in schedule works for both parties, without having to call from a business meeting, crowded subway, or that crazy traffic jam.

Don't underestimate the effect of such textual attention. It is oftentimes the little things piling up that can derail an otherwise healthy relationship. Instead of seeming like an irresponsible, or worse yet, uncaring person who feels her own schedule is more important than respecting her partner's time, you can demonstrate that you not only respect your companion's time, but also care enough to make the effort to go the extra mile. Sure, maybe five more minutes and you'll be there anyhow. But if you put a preprogrammed message in there such as, "running late, will be there in a few minutes, sorry!" you can send your communication off with abandon, and earn huge karmic points with your partner in the process. No one likes feeling taken for granted, and these simple steps can go a long way.

There are many other simple acts you can take to achieve the same goals. If you're stopping at the store on the way home, try dropping a quick text to see if he needs anything. Or what about when you've decided to crash at a friend's house? A quick TM to your guy to let him know you're safe and sound is a great way to stay textually connected. Same goes for when your flight lands safely at your destination, or when the boss has just given you a raise but you're not free to call. All these little things make for great textual updates if within the context of a healthy relationship, and if sent for legitimate reasons when you're honest with yourself on the deepest levels.

Doesn't it feel wonderful when someone considers your needs too? Of course it does! And so long as you have taken the steps listed in the prior chapter to really assess your motives for texting, and are doing these things for the right reasons, not simply for attention or because you're feeling insecure, these little acts of textual consideration can go a long way toward creating not only a wonderful text life, but a wonderful life overall.

▁▃▅▇ Textual Implants

KNOW YOUR GUY IS heading into a particularly challenging day? This is the time to let him know you offer the support and understanding he has always longed for. A well-timed, well-chosen message can plant you firmly in his heart and mind as his font of endless strength and encouragement, much the way other kinds of implants can place other elements of you firmly in his mind's eye. ;)

Again, if you've embarked on healthy, balanced textual exploration, you know better than to fall into overtexting, but you also know that there are moments when a short, supportive text can change his day for the better.

Is he heading in to face a performance review? To ask for that raise? To pitch the big deal? To take that big test? A texty cheer from the sidelines could boost his ego and his confidence. Sending a short, quick TM with a "go get 'em" feel to it can go a long way toward lending him support and letting him know you're there for him.

The trick is to deliver it in a way that demonstrates you've got total confidence in him, rather than that you think he needs all the luck he can get.

There are also ways in which you can help him look great and for which he may well be appreciative. Has he been under a lot of stress this past week, and maybe not as focused on things as he normally would be? A quick TM to remind him of an upcoming event such as "Mother's Day is this weekend" could be greatly appreciated. You can even be a real friend and let him know it without letting on that you suspected he needed reminding. How so? A quick TM of, "Whew, finally found the perfect thing to send my mom for Mother's Day this weekend!" could serve to trigger his memory without making him feel like a mess-up. We can all use a little friendly reminder once in a while, and we all enjoy receiving that help in a way that doesn't bruise our ego. Your trusty little textual habits can help make that happen in the classiest, most supportive ways possible. Wouldn't you want others to do the same for you?

This isn't about being the perfect girlfriend, or playing some kind of game. It is about finding ways to be supportive and kind to those in your life. No one is telling you to be a doormat or subservient—think of the old Golden Rule, "Do unto others as you would have them do unto you." Wouldn't you be appreciative of such things? Well, in all likelihood your partner would too. However, once again, make sure you are doing so to be genuinely helpful and considerate, not just to "catch" him. A good catch does not a good mate make, if he was caught deceptively! Besides, wouldn't you rather have him getting worked up over how to catch you, amazing girl that you are? Of course you would, and it is through little things like consideration and paying attention to your intentions when you communicate with him that go a long way to demonstrating just who you are, and what you can be in his life.

One caveat if you choose to perform little helps such as these for him. Never, ever, ever throw back in his face at an angry moment, "I've done all these things for you!" Remember, you are doing them out of the goodness of your heart, out of your genuine consideration for helping another out as you would want to be helped out in return. All of these suggestions are, after all, operating from the premise that you are in a healthy, balanced, two-way relationship! If you're not, you need to be focusing on why you're there and what to do about it, not on serving someone else's needs. Remember, too, that this is a two-way street; hopefully you will demonstrate to your partner how to support you, too. If he sees you operating with high integrity in your interactions, supporting and enjoying him, as opposed to trying to "catch" him, or nagging or obsessing over him, he will be far more likely to perform these same supportive actions for you.

Keep in mind, too, that no matter how "helpful" you are, if the relationship isn't working, you can jump through hoops, and it still isn't likely to work. However, if your relationship is overall relatively healthy, but you would appreciate a little help keeping yourself on his mind when he's away, you could find such textual implants can truly make a difference.

▄▄■■ Textual Cues

DO YOU HAVE THE MEMORY of a goldfish? Ever forget an important engagement, or that your (hopefully) future mother-in-law is coming into town? Setting up textual cues with the calendar features on your cell phone can greatly enhance your relations.

In this instance, I'm not talking about the TMs you send him, but more about the reminders you send yourself, utilizing the calendar and reminder features on your cell phone. Attention to detail and scheduling can enhance a relationship. Make notes about important events in your own life and your partner's. Don't just note calendar events, but also his mood, or different things that happened that day. This can also help you uncover patterns. Does he always get moodier two days before a big meeting? Is he always more relaxed after he goes for a run?

This information that you can record in your calendar and note pages can help you create a smoother relationship once you analyze the patterns—patterns your partner may not even realize he has! If you notice he's calmer after a run, you know that this is the best time to let him know your parents are coming to town. You also know those two days before a big meeting are not the best times to spring such information on him, as he's unduly stressed at that time.

You can also use these cues to help you both out. If you understand that pattern of stress before the big meetings, you can choose low-key activities for those times, which can contribute to making your overall time together far more pleasurable for both of you.

Of course, you can also use your cell phone features for basic things like not forgetting his birthday, or to remind you that the Super Bowl is next week—a.k.a., spa day with the girls (or, if you enjoy the game, to buy extra chips for the big party you two will be hosting together!). These are only a few of the ways a clever gal can begin to utilize her cell phone to cue her in to creating a better, stronger relationship. Planning and attention to intention can help you create an amazing life, in text and outside of it. And just a hint here: this can work for YOU, too. We all have patterns of which we aren't aware. If you make calendar notes of your own life, you may discover that you always feel sleepy or moody after a particular meal, activity, or project. If you learn to uncover these patterns, you can master them, and then you are in control of far more of your life than you otherwise would be. Who would've thought your trusty little cell phone could be the key to such power in your own life, and in your relationship?

▄▂▆▉ Fore-Text

WOMEN ARE KNOWN TO complain about lack of foreplay in their sex lives. Well, that little vibrating wonder in your pocket can help spice up your love life in more ways than one! Want to set the stage for a bombastic evening of torrid passion? Start with a long, slow buildup that grows more intense throughout the day. A little taste of the joy he will experience when he next sees you can keep him eagerly awaiting.

While many women assume this means naughty text messages, it need not. Anything that arouses his interest can leave him hungry for more of your time and attention. And the more you strike this chord in him, the more he is likely to respond and satisfy your needs for attention.

Another reason to keep the naughty messages to a minimum is that you don't want to make the teaser better than the actual show. Sometimes if we build things up too much, it can cause pressure on one or both sides. The idea is to provide a little teaser and then step back, engrossing yourself again in the business of your day, a bit unavailable. Again, make him work for it. This is not manipulation, this is seduction. Very different things! You are raising the ante, upping your value. If he comes home knowing you will be waiting there for him at his beck and call, he can come in and feel totally comfortable sitting down and grabbing a few beers while he watches TV as you make dinner, as he reads the paper or plays with the dog, responding to whatever you say with "uh huh, yeah honey, whatever you say . . ."—knowing you're there whenever he's ready.

Sounds spicy, doesn't it? I don't think so! Wouldn't a better scenario be one where he practically runs through the door, eager to get to you; you're all he's thought about all afternoon!

He can't wait to take you into his arms, his mouth eagerly finding yours after you whisper to him a reference to this afternoon's textual intercourse. He sweeps you up into his arms, ready to ravish you. His desire for you has been building all day. He feels like the luckiest man in the world to have you to come home to.

Maybe you don't even respond right away. Maybe you suggest you cook some dinner together and he eagerly agrees, trying to flirt and seduce you as you're peeling the carrots, hoping that the two of you will sizzle as much as the food in that frying pan. The truth is, he can't even think of food right now, he wants you so badly. Now the game is in your hands. He's the one wanting more. You control the pace and the flow. And when he finally does get you in his arms, his passion is incredible, as is yours, because he's been giving you his full attention, and paid attention to your needs.

What made the difference? Through your teasery, you created a way for him to have to win you over all over again. You managed from afar to create stimulating fore-text that has led up to a far more satisfying scenario than you might otherwise be experiencing.

▁▄█ Quickie Text

THERE ARE TIMES WHEN YOU'RE simply too busy to talk, so you need a quick answer on the fly. Such moments were made for texting! Short, succinct messages can make life go more smoothly, helping you navigate through everyday life flawlessly, all while learning that yes, he does like the idea of a postmodern sofa, and of course you can pick it out yourself, without truly taking him away from his work or game.

Quickie text is also ideal for determining tonight's dinner, coordinating meeting time and location, or making a change in plans. Quickie text can go a long way toward creating smoother, more fulfilling relationships. Keep them short and to the point. These TMs are designed to be informational only, though you may want to add an emoticon or "XO" once in a while.

Remember, though, this kind of quickie text refers to changes in plans, not actually setting up a date. If you are new to a relationship, you really should train your man to ask you out in advance. He shouldn't expect you to be available on a whim, or in the middle of the night. That can set a bad precedent for the future, one that could leave you in a constant state of anxiety, never feeling truly honored and respected. Texting has changed the dynamic of the booty call completely, making it feel safer than ever for a man to try to text you up. Make him earn that right. If he has to earn your time and attention, he will respect and appreciate it a lot more.

It all comes back again to the intentions behind your textual intercourse, on both the sending and the receiving end. If you are looking for a serious relationship, make sure you set the pace from the beginning for him to treat yours like a serious relationship. The advent of text messaging has allowed way too many men out there to feel they no longer have to act like gentlemen. However, a savvy girl in control of her textual relationships knows better. She knows that if she wants to stand out from the crowd, she is going to demonstrate that she expects his respect.

You can see, then, that while quickie text can help make you more accessible in order to create a smoother, more balanced and connected relationship, it can also do the opposite, creating an anxiety-ridden relationship where you are never sure where you stand, as he takes your ever-readiness for granted. So use quickie text wisely, and use it well. In this book you will learn many ways in which to set boundaries so that you can harness your textual powers to create tremendous good in your relationship.

Textual Prophylactics

Personal and physical safety is tremendously important, especially in this ever more violent world. That safety extends to your text life too. There are many aspects of our textual safety to consider, ranging from avoiding textual stalkers to avoiding distasteful spam-text—to avoiding texting and driving at all costs!

First and foremost, be careful whom you give access to your textual self. When you open yourself up textually, you should consider how well you know the person. Many girls can relate the story of a guy who seemed totally fine but after a few days of anonymous textual intercourse suddenly sprang an overly racy textual message on them out of the blue.

To prevent text stalking, you may be better off giving out a landline or work phone number as opposed to your cell. You should also avoid giving your cell number online or to businesses that may spam you—at your own expense! Think before you give the world easy textual access.

To ensure your physical safety while texting, don't text and drive! Far too many people are injured or killed in car accidents because of this hazardous form of text messaging. When a driver takes her eyes off the road, even for a few seconds, the distraction delays her response time to cars, signs, traffic lights, and other road obstacles. Don't risk somebody's life or your own.

Chapter 3

Reaching Your Textual Peak

CONFIDENCE CAN BE GAINED with the mastery of any skill, and it is no different with text messaging. With a little bit of education and some practice, your textual confidence will rise in no time. Not only will you know how to send stimulating textual messages, but you'll know that when you do so, you are moving your relationship yet another step closer toward meeting the one of your dreams. If you want to reach your textual peak, you will need to become textually confident. So, read on!

The Ins and Outs of
Textual Intercourse

THE FIRST STEP TO BUILDING confidence in any new endeavor is to gain a clear understanding of "the rules of the game." In textual intercourse, that would involve knowing the rules of text-iquette: When is it appropriate to text? When should you pick up the phone, and when should you meet in person? What should you do if his message is unclear? How much can you say in text without crossing a line? What do you do if a text message goes astray? What should you do if he doesn't respond? What if he gets overly textual or sends inappropriate messages? What about textual fidelity? How much text is too much text? How much text is too little?

Once you explore and acknowledge your textual preferences and accept that your goals in the bigger picture can help you determine whether your intentions in your handling of each individual TM—outgoing and incoming alike—are helping you meet those goals, you will have gone a long way toward building confidence during textual intercourse, as you'll see in the following chapters.

The reality is that while there is proper protocol, people do in fact violate rules of etiquette all the time, and without tremendous repercussions. However, for you this will be different. You will be examining the rules of text-iquette through the filter of your own goals, and that will further empower you in making decisions, and in mastering the art of textual intercourse in the deepest, most intimate of ways—ways that reflect who you are and that bring you closer to being the pure reflection of who you want to be in your interactions with others.

Once you've done this, you simply go on to learn the basic techniques of etiquette, so that you understand the nuts and bolts of delivering the message you truly want to send, in a way that it will be received clearly and concisely. Once you acknowledge your true intentions behind your textual communications and master the nuances, you will find that you can navigate the textual landscape easily, while avoiding the textual landmines so many others stumble into. Why? Because you will be utilizing your greater goals, that clear understanding of your intentions behind your textual attentions which raises the nuance of every interaction you have to the highest level possible, helping you create a stellar text life, and relationship, alike.

..∎∎ Text Talk

EVERY INTEREST IN LIFE SEEMS TO be accompanied by its own language, terms, and expressions specific to that interest. When it comes to textuality, that language is spoken in abbreviated code. In addition to learning the many nuances of textual intercourse, it feels almost as if you have to learn a foreign language! To complicate things further, this language has many dialects. While there are many abbreviations which are common knowledge, such as "c u l8er" meaning "see you later," there are others that people might make up as they go along, and the meanings can be very different from one party to the next.

Additionally, people can act in ways that just seem brash or inconsiderate to you, even though it seems perfectly natural to them. For instance, Julia had a boyfriend who knew she was at an event where she couldn't text—she was serving as a bridesmaid in a wedding, one he couldn't attend due to his work schedule. It didn't seem to matter to him that she was serving in a ceremony. He kept texting her throughout the whole night, almost as if he was competing with the event! However, when she confronted him about it later, he was crushed that she saw it as obsessive and inappropriate. He felt he was working hard to keep them connected. He thought it was a way to still be there, when he couldn't be there physically. I'm sure you can guess that things like this happen all the time. What one person will think a totally natural action, another will be horrified by.

These kinds of texty situations can create many pitfalls in the textual world. One element of building confidence will be learning to remember to always ask yourself, what is my intention in this communication? If you are on the receiving end of the message, stop and ask yourself, what do I think his intention is in this? If you are uncertain about the answer, ask!

If Julia had stopped and asked herself, what is his intention? she might have been able to go from feeling stunned at the apparent intrusion of his insisting on TM at a time that was inappropriate, to thinking, perhaps there is something else going on here, and he's just picking a poor way to express it. Granted, that may not be the case; he could just be spoiled and self-important. However, if Julia felt bad enough about it, the best thing to do would be to express it, and to ask him directly about the situation. In order to have healthy, solid textual communications, you must take the extra step of ensuring clarity on both sides of the conversation.

▁▂▃▅ Setting Textual Boundaries

All successful communication requires boundaries that maximize the comfort level of all parties, and the same is true of textual communication. When we set boundaries we are marking out an arena within which we can communicate safely. Those rules, or boundaries, rather than restricting us, can actually create a greater freedom. Once we know what is and is not acceptable, we are free to dive in confidently. There is a gift in knowing that so long as you adhere to A, B, and C, anything goes. It unleashes within you the ability to push the limits, to take risks knowing that they are safe, as you already know clearly what is out of bounds.

Far too often people see boundaries as restrictive, not realizing the tremendous freedom they create. If you begin doing this with TM, you will soon grow to see how powerful this method is, and you may even want to consider setting clear boundaries in other areas of your life. See chapter 5 to learn what kinds of boundaries you can consider defining, and how to go about setting them. Why would you need to do this with something as basic as text messages? OBSESSION. People can express their obsession via text messaging, in numerous ways.

Listen to Erik's story: "I dated a girl for two years who became *obsessed* with texting. So obsessed, in fact, that I had to make a rule that she was only allowed to text me ten times during a business day while I was at work. She never followed that rule, and I easily got over one hundred texts a day while at work. These texts included questions like, are you seeing someone else? Did you ever cheat on me? Who are you with right now? As you can guess, the relationship ended."

You will want to make sure you know how to handle the textually obsessed, and boundaries will help you do it, and help you notice when they begin to become obsessed, rather than only coming to realize it when they are over the top. Furthermore, if you follow my suggestions to focus on your intentions for texting, you will be able to avoid accidentally becoming one of the textually obsessed yourself!

▬▪▪▮ *Always Practice Safe Text*

As with any sport or activity, texting has its own rules for safe text. Skipping the prophylactics could mean you wind up being text-stalked, suffering textual molestation, or textual humiliation. Once you know you've taken every precaution to keep yourself physically and emotionally safe during textual intercourse, as well as keeping your cell phone free from communicable textual diseases, you will feel far more confident about your text life.

BE TEXTUALLY SELECTIVE

How do you go about that? I know you're probably a free-wheeling, fun-loving kind of girl, but when you meet someone new, be cautious about opening up your whole world to them. Handing out your cell number, and subsequently full textual access, opens you up to a constant stream of unguarded interaction. Many people feel comfortable sending TMs at times they would never consider calling. When you hand your number to a guy you meet at a party or in a bar, for instance, don't be too surprised when he begins to TM you when he's had a few too many drinks and worked up some courage. That same guy might think twice about calling at a late hour, but TMing you? Nah. It feels innocuous. So, before you hand out your number to just anyone, consider that you don't know them and you could be handing your number to your next text stalker!

What's a girl to do? Try giving him your e-mail, instant messaging screen name, work number, or landline, at least until you know him better. That keeps you safe from round-the-clock access by every Tom, Dick, and Harry that you meet. Well, unless you're into that sort of thing.

USE TEXTUAL PROTECTION

Another hazard in the textual world is textually transmitted diseases, otherwise known as cell phone viruses. These pesky little things can cost you money, screw up your icons, and cause you lots of headaches. You can avoid them by installing anti-virus protection on your cell phone such as that by McAfee or F-Secure. You also want to disable the *open* on your Bluetooth or Personal Digital Assistant, such as a PalmPilot, as these are oftentimes access routes for common viruses. Keep an eye on your bill, too, for unusual charges. These may be a tip-off of a nasty little infection. All it takes is a few simple steps to keep you and your cell phone safe and sound, a small price to pay for great textual health!

Chapter 4

Basic Text-iquette

ALL COMMUNICATION HAS RULES OF ETIQUETTE, whether they are spoken or not. These rules allow for comfortable, safe, engaging communication wherein people are encouraged to enjoy open rapport. They can also prevent one from experiencing excruciating embarrassment!

We have already explored the concept of textual confidence, so you know that having a firm grip on the rules of great text will help you strip away the feelings of self-doubt and textual insecurity. We will begin by looking at when one should and should not textually paw at her partner. From there, we will examine the concept of respecting textual boundaries, quickie text, handling textual molestation, the concept of surrogate texting, and much more!

▗▄▌ Textually Charged

THERE ARE TIMES THAT clearly call for text messaging, so much so that they seem textually charged. Perhaps you are stuck in that meeting, yet are expected to be on the way to dinner. Or perhaps you need to send a good luck message to someone about to step on stage to accept an award. A quick, quiet text lets them know they are in your thoughts, or updates them on your situation at times when you may not be able to call.

This is where TM really shines, allowing you to be there and be supportive at times when you otherwise could not. Getting a good handle on the times and circumstances wherein it is not only advisable, but almost mandatory to text, is a great step toward a solid and highly functional text life.

When are text messages ideal? Any of the following situations can be a great opportunity for stroking off some good vibrations:
- running late
- a change in plans
- a quick thank-you message after a casual event
- a cheery hello when you know someone is down, but you don't have time to call
- when you want to keep connected but are tied up with work, school, or some other activity
- when you need directions
- to send an address or other specific information to some-

one who may not have a pen handy

- when updating your friends or loved one on a quick piece of information not relevant enough to require a phone call, but important enough to share

▃▃▊▊ Inappropriate Text

MUCH AS THERE ARE TIMES when it is highly appropriate to text, there are times when fingering your phone is a no-no! Even though you may feel an overwhelming drive to act, and can barely keep your hands to yourself, these situations call for restraint! Remember, pay attention to your intention. Are you *that girl* or are you an *it girl*? Anyone can send a cowardly, angry text. However, a woman in control of her life and her emotions doesn't send off something based on an emotion alone. She can have that emotion; it is natural to. However, she doesn't succumb to it. Instead, she has her eyes on the prize: becoming who she wants to be in the world. She knows that by being an amazing partner, she attracts an amazing partner. She also knows that if she is less than that person she knows herself to be, she won't hold on to a great partner for very long. So she acts accordingly, choosing to think twice before sending off a text, ensuring that she has paid attention to her intention behind writing it, and asking herself if it serves her greater good in the big picture.

⌁⌁▮▮ *Practicing Good Clean Text*

NO MATTER HOW JUST you feel your cause to be, it isn't fair play to text your boyfriend an angry, instigating message when you know he's in a meeting with the boss, or cannot otherwise respond to you. It is equally poor form to deliver upsetting information when you know someone cannot react without embarrassment, or cannot contact you back.

Yes, we've already acknowledged earlier that you may have good reason to be angry at him. You may even feel that for your own well-being, you MUST get this out NOW, not later. That is why the best way to handle such texting is to develop your own "code of behavior" for texting when you are feeling calm. If you do so, you will at least have guidelines in place for yourself when a situation does arise. You may not want to adhere to them at that point, but they will at least be there in the back of your mind, reminding you that the "you" that you are when not angry would not choose this course of action. In other chapters you will learn how to handle this situation. For now, however, let's look at situations where it would just be dirty, no-good texting for you to give in to your baser desire to "let him have it now!" Those would include:

- **Setting:** This is when you know he is in a situation where others will notice if he is reading something upsetting.

Think: work meetings, presentations, a big game, a wedding or other event (that you may be angry you aren't attending), a class, an exam, at a dinner, traveling. The chapter on *Textual Warfare* will help you better understand the many ways in which this behavior is actually dangerous to the very credibility of your relationship, and to your sense of integrity to self.

- **Availability:** If you send an angry message when you know he can't "get into it" or respond, it's just plain unfair. Imagine how you'd feel were you bombarded with angry, provocative messages that got you more upset by the minute, but you weren't in a position to respond to them, much less defend yourself.

- **Taste:** Some things are just wrong to text. These include all the topics listed in *Inappropriate Text*. It is important to understand that violating the rules of taste when texting not only is dirty, it can undermine who you are in his eyes, and even in your own. Don't fight dirty.

What are some rules you may want to make for yourself, in order to help you practice good clean text?

HANDLING TEXTUAL MOLESTATION

You've taken great pains to practice good textual prophylactics, but someone has surprised you, nonetheless. All of a sudden it happens. You thrill at the sudden vibration heralding a
new message filled with textual promise only to open it up to
suffer a terrible textual disappointment: a truly offensive
textual assault.

Perhaps the perpetrator is an eager would-be suitor who
has been out drinking with the boys and decides to go for it
in TM. If it doesn't work, he figures he can always apologize
later for a drunken error.

Never, ever accept drunkenness as an excuse for such
behavior. If someone oversteps his bounds when drunk, he is
only doing what he didn't quite have the nerve to do when
sober. This man obviously doesn't realize that he has to earn
the right to take that next step with you, and if he is to take it
at all, it should be through making an attempt to kiss you at
the end of a date, not by sending you an unexpected,
unprecedented raunchy text.

If your goal is a relationship, then you need to draw the
boundaries now, and clearly. Nip it right in the bud, responding with something like, "I M offended, who do u think u r

talking 2? Do Not Contact Me Again." Don't tell yourself you want contact again if he can behave better. He has already demonstrated he lacks proper respect for you and doesn't even have the decency to approach you in a proper context. Any boy (a real man wouldn't do this!) who is willing to make crude comments to you in text, with no prior reason to believe this is acceptable, does not deserve your time and attention, no matter how wonderful he otherwise may seem, or how attracted you otherwise are to him. Hold out for the best, and that applies to the best text, too.

If you decided to forgive him, then be aware this will likely dictate a future pattern in your relationship, which may not be a relationship so much as an ongoing string of booty calls!

.. ▮▮ Textual Respect

YOU ARE OUT ON A DATE having a wonderful time, and suddenly you feel the vibration in your pocket. What do you do? I mean, no biggie if you check it real quick, right?

You may want to think twice before whipping out your cell to check the message unless you have an important reason to, such as that it may be your boss, an ill parent or child at home, or something equally compelling. Yes, it has become widely accepted and people have been forced to live with the realities of in-your-face textuality; however, if you are out with someone you truly care for, ask yourself yet again, what is my intention behind spending time with this person? If it is to enjoy his company, or to get to know him better, or to build strong bonds with him, is that really going to happen if you spend the whole night fondling your cell?

It really boils down to respect, for both the person you are out with and the party texting you. Does either really get your full focus and attention when you are multitasking your time and attentions? So often we complain about the lack of quality in our relationships, but ignore the ways in which we ourselves act to degrade that quality.

Have you thought about how your date feels when you make interruptions from your friends more important than his dinner conversation? Who knows what he was about to disclose? For all you know he's been thinking you are the girl of his dreams, and is trying to work up the courage to tell you that when—there you go—back on the cell again. Does he really trust, too, that it is one of your ever-present girlfriends? Or does he wonder, secretly, if it is some other guy? If he does believe it's your girlfriends, think about this: Just as he's trying to envision a life spent with wonderful you, there go your girls interrupting his time again. How romantic can his vision of your life together get if he now has to imagine it as constantly interrupted by friends whose needs seem more important than time with him?

I recommend you again visit the intentions of your actions, and who and how you want to be not just textually, but in all your interactions with others. Are your choices and actions supporting it? Think carefully before you automatically text while out with others. People have survived dates for millennia without the aid of a cell phone, much less TM. If your goal is a healthy, bonded relationship, check in with yourself before you check out of conversation with him in order to read another TM.

◾◾◾ Textual Obsession

WE'VE ALL BEEN THERE: You sent a tremendously witty or playful message and eagerly awaited the response . . . but . . . nothing! You check and recheck to make sure you sent your text to the right address. You decide maybe it didn't go through, and you perhaps dare to send it again. Oh, the confusion! It is enough to drive a girl mad!

So you text your girls and ask them what to do. Each time one texts you back, you are hoping it is him, but of course it isn't. Your mind begins to wander, running over all the possible reasons he has failed to respond. You start wondering what you did wrong. You go over everything you said and did last time you were together. You go back and read over prior texts. You start wondering what could be wrong. Were you too forward? Were you too clingy? No, wait, maybe you didn't show him how much he means to you! In fact, you can fix this, you decide! You will show him how awesome you are. You are going to reclaim this!

But wait . . . maybe . . . he just didn't get the text? You decide to resend it. And you wait. An hour goes by, then two. No response. Okay, back to the other plan. You are going to show him how awesome you are. In fact, you are going to demonstrate to him how understanding you are that he didn't write back. So you text him one—nope, not enough room; it crosses over into two TMs—telling him how understanding you are that he was obviously too busy to respond. You smile to yourself. Yes, indeed, you've now thoughtfully demonstrated that you understand he has other things going on.

Wow, sounds rational on the surface, huh? But what did he really receive? First of all, he may have been legitimately busy. Or perhaps he was in a bad mood over something that had NOTHING to do with you. Instead of putting that negative energy into his response, he decided to wait to respond to you later.

However, then he gets a resend, and he's starting to feel pressured. You've again taken time from his busy schedule, or if he was in that bad mood, well, now he's feeling *really* pressured.

Then your "understanding" message comes through, and he reads that as your being passive aggressive, telling him he is obviously too busy for you. Instead of seeing that as helpful, he is feeling terrified of the woman who is textually obsessed with him. So, when in reality he might have been excited to find the time to respond to you a little later, instead, he now wants to avoid you. He's also wondering why you have so much time on your hands. *Does she have no life?* he wonders.

See how quickly an obsessive text—a text sent without paying attention to your intention, and making sure that the action was in alignment with who you are at core—can spiral into exactly the opposite of what you hope to accomplish? Don't be an obsessive texter. If someone hasn't responded to you within twenty-four hours, you can try dropping them another line. If you don't hear back from him by then, and you are in a relationship where you normally would, you can either pick up the phone and ask directly, or, my preference, get busy with your own life. When he finally does make an appearance, let him know that it was no big deal; you've been busy too.

He will set to wondering what you were so busy with that you didn't go into a panic over him. He will wonder why you didn't behave like other girls, texting obsessively. He will wonder how you could live without him like that. And *that* will make him want to learn more about you. Doesn't that work more toward fulfilling your desired goals than scaring him off through obsessive texting? If you cannot stop yourself from texting him, write the text and save it. DO NOT SEND IT. Write it one hundred different times and erase each one, saving only one in the *save* folder. And later, delete that one too. Make him text you up. You will soon discover that he is so disconcerted over the fact that you aren't hunting him down (which makes you look like a very cool girl indeed, and a prize to be won above all others), that he will be the one filling your box with his bulging text.

What could you do rather than text him when it's unnecessary, or when it doesn't add to your life or your relationship to do so?

▪▪▪▪ Surrogate Texting

HOURS HAVE PASSED BY and you haven't heard a response, or worse, it's been days! You begin to beg and plead with a mutual friend to step up to bat and put in a text for your cause. You know she can do it, she's friends with him too, but you also know he will likely catch on to what's going on. But what else is a girl to do? I mean, you could lose your mind waiting for him to get back to you.

As it is, you've again analyzed the situation from every angle. You tried resending the message. You may even have sent the "extra-support" message. Other than driving over to his house and flinging yourself at him, what else can you do but call in the aid of a mutual friend? Asking a friend to send a teensy weensy TM to him to see what's up is nothing, not even a mole-hill, much less a mountain.

Kid yourself not, my friend! It is a mountain, a big scary mountain in his eyes. If you proceed with this one, you will validate any doubts he may have had that delayed his response to begin with. Somebody who likes you will be willing to move mountains. The reality is he may have simply been busy. But on the other hand, when a man is infatuated, he has a funny way of being able to manufacture all the time he needs to pur-sue the object of his desire. One of two things could be going on here:

1. You made it too easy for him; there is no more hunt left in the game. You are now easily obtained, and he has begun to take you for granted, or worse, maybe even lost interest.

2. He may just not be as into you as you are into him. Both problems employ the same solution. Put him out of your mind, busy up your life with all sorts of fantastic you-building activities: go to the gym; take a course; get together with friends; learn a new hobby—you know the routine. Make your life fantastic. And, in the process, he'll wonder where you went. He's used to the routine by now. When he starts treating a girl this way, she usually ups the ante: calling and TMing

more; jumping through hoops to meet his every need. But now . . . now you are different; you are standing out. You have disappeared off his radar. One of two things will happen: He will forget you entirely, and if a man finds you that easily forgettable, he is *so not* a man worth having. You deserve a man who finds you priceless beyond compare. You deserve a man who sees you as the rarest gem in the world, unlike any other. The man you deserve *will* move mountains for you—if you don't scare him away first, which, you hopefully realize by now, some of our behaviors before we began to think intentionally were apt to do.

The second thing that could happen? He begins to panic when he notices you aren't responding in the same way as girls from his past. Have I lost my mojo? he begins to wonder. Wow, you must have tons of suitors lined up if you could forget about him so quickly, he will think. What have they discovered about you that he has yet to uncover? He begins to wonder, and suddenly the tables turn, and he reappears, pursuing you hotter than ever.

So, back to our question: When is it okay to call in a surrogate texter? Whenever you don't care to have him around for a long time; whenever you don't mind being just like all the rest, a girl he will likely discard once he gets bored with the easy access; or when you honestly, truly believe something bad (like death, destruction) may have happened to him, but don't want to be so forward as to contact him directly again yourself. But let's be honest here. If you have a mutual friend, you would already know if the tragedy struck, right? Right-o. So, let's go with the answer being: Never. Make him come to you, or write him off, and say "next!" I also want you to tell yourself something: "If he can't step up, then I want someone better!" Make that your mantra. If a man cannot step up, he does not deserve you. Period. No ifs, ands, or buts about it. You can send him a million TMs and that won't change a thing. If he cannot do right by you, if you have to jump through textual hoops to get him, he just isn't worth having no matter how amazing you think he is.

▄▄▌▌ Textual Discrimination

THINK BEFORE YOU TEXT! What if his phone is lying on his desk and a coworker sees the message? Worse still, what if his mom does?

I've spoken throughout of the importance of thinking about how and when your text is received, and paying attention to your intention, and making sure that your true intention in sending this text aligns with your overall goals of who you are, who you want to be, and how you are perceived. Now, however, we are going to talk of something else: discretion. Discretion according to its most basic meaning.

Yes, you may text him for myriad reasons, and so long as you aren't sacrificing who you really are simply by following a momentary emotion, all should be fine, right? Theoretically this is true. If he cannot handle who you are, or the choices you make when you are most honestly being your truest self, then he probably isn't the right partner for you. However, so far you've texted with care to paying attention to your intention, and things are going wonderfully. Never has your text life or your romance been better.

Until . . . something goes wrong. Remember, much as we try to be discreet, one never knows where a text could wind up. First, there is human error to consider: you hit the wrong name in your address book and suddenly you're telling your brother how hot you are for him. OUCH! There is also the fact that you never know where your guy's phone is at the moment. Perhaps he left it in the dugout while he's up at bat. Maybe a nosy team-mate picks it up and reads your message.

Worse still, he's visiting the folks and his phone's on the table while he's in the other room. Maybe his mom, sibling, or nephew picks up the phone and glances at his incoming message. OUCH!

Yes, it's an invasion of privacy. You can even get mad at him for not guarding his cell phone, but is that fair? Can you protect your messages at every moment of every day? You cannot,

not unless you take the time and make the effort to set a pass-code that must be entered to read text or answer the phone. Most people forgo this, seeing it as too much of a hassle, and it can be, if you receive an awful lot of text or calls.

The bottom line is, though, that you cannot expect the person on the other end always to be totally in control of who may glance at a message. Could you promise that one of your own girlfriends, family members, or coworkers would NEVER try to sneak a glance at an incoming message? You can make best efforts, but best efforts can be thwarted by nosy people.

You can hope he doesn't have such people in his life, and if he can manage that, it is wonderful. But we all know how friends can tease, or family members can snoop. So, before you send off a message you could regret later, just pause a moment and make sure you would be comfortable knowing that others could see it. And also ask yourself for a moment, how will he feel if someone else reads it? Will he laugh it off? Be embarrassed? It is always good to check in with others before getting too suggestive in TM. Remember, while it is likely no one but your intended will see the TM, it isn't a guarantee. Make your decision to send accordingly!

Preventing Textual Humiliation

There is nothing quite like the embarrassment of mistakenly sending Aunt Hilda a message about how you can't wait to get her into bed tonight, except the embarrassment of sending the office hottie the message inquiring as to how Aunt Hilda's hemorrhoids are doing. Textual misdirection and premature textuation (sending a message before you have clarification) are two of the many ways to find yourself textually humiliated.

When sending a text message you want to always double check the recipient. Sometimes in the heat of fast-paced texting you can accidentally send to the wrong person, especially if new messages come in while you are TMing someone else.

If you pay attention to your intention and review your message before hitting *send* you will also have taken that extra moment to double check the recipient. See that? If you step away from the frenzy of textual obsession, and focus on the intentions and goals of your textual intercourse, not only will you have far better textual experiences, but you will reduce your risk of textual humiliation, too!

Chapter 5

Textual Boundaries

AT ONE TIME OR ANOTHER MOST OF US have experienced that overzealous boy who couldn't seem to accept that we didn't want to go out with him, no matter how many times we rejected him. Time and again he'd ask, going over the top in his efforts to impress us. Or what about the new boyfriend who, much as we enjoyed his attentions, could be a bit overwhelming in his expression of them? Or what of the overly needy friend or lover who doesn't understand that there are times when it is just inappropriate to call or show up unannounced?

In the textual world we can be victims of equally overwhelming amorous attentions, sometimes more so as people feel safer in sending an appeal that is somewhat anonymous, at least in that they don't have to face you directly, much less hear indignation in your voice as they would on the phone. TM can make someone feel less intimidated in risking saying something a bit risqué for the first time, or contacting you at an otherwise indecent hour. Not to mention the overly texty guy who, if his attention is unwanted, can quite possibly turn into a textual stalker. Even if this guy isn't exactly dangerous, he can be quite a nuisance.

Much as you may welcome such attentions from the right person, it goes back to: What is your goal? Do you want to be his *right now* girl, or his *one and only girl*? If you just want a casual fling, then by all means go ahead, but if what you want is a relationship as opposed to being his "friend with benefits," you have to stop the casual feeling of constant access that TM can create in dealing with a new beau, reserving it for interaction that creates a stronger relationship rather than succumbing to late night booty calls, or becoming the girl he can get on a moment's notice.

For these reasons, as well as for our safety when dating someone new to us, it is important to set clear textual boundaries. Equally important is creating boundaries that ensure we don't become textually obsessed. This chapter will explore ways in which you can do this.

▪▪▮▮ Defining Your Textual Limits

THE FIRST STEP IN ESTABLISHING BOUNDARIES with others is

making sure we understand our own textual limits. Sometimes we can be wishy-washy about our boundaries. Don't be. This can wreak all sorts of textual havoc! If you are okay with three a.m. texts or naughty messages one day, you cannot decide the next day that you aren't. You need to decide for yourself what you are okay with, and then make that message clear to others.

To begin to determine your own boundaries, let's revisit the earlier sections on the pros and cons of casual text. What are you seeking from your interaction? Are you looking for a casual relationship or a lasting love? If this is just a casual thing, remember that the guy might be more interested in your sexual technique than your texual technique. They may appreciate some of what you will learn in the chapter on *Hot Text!*

Who do you want to be? How do you want him to perceive you? Revisit some of your answers in *Textual Preference*. If you want to be more than some mere textual adventure, or flavor of the month, you have to keep him on his game. Stir up the hunter in him, as we discussed earlier. Boundaries are an important key to achieving this.

So let's walk through the process. A girl who already has a happy, fulfilling life of her own, who wants a man who respects, honors, cherishes, and adores her—what kind of behavior on his part would fit that bill? Would she have to chase him down? Would he keep her dangling, wondering if she would see him again, or would he be on top of it, and already letting her know when they will see each other again? He certainly wouldn't wait until the middle of the night to call her and see if she is available. He won't risk the possibility that she won't be, or that someone else is getting to her first. If you let him know you are indeed available at such hours, you take away any concern he has that someone else will steal your heart in the meantime. *And* you create the feeling that you may make yourself so easily available to whoever else shows up. Guys want to feel that the girl who likes them does so because they are special. Don't let him feel ordinary, or like you're willing to hand yourself away without any effort on his part. If he cares, if he is a guy worth his salt, he will rise to the occasion. If he doesn't, he probably isn't worth having around.

Would the girl deserving of the love you long for be wondering if he thought of her today? No way. He'd be calling or TMing her with his thoughts. If he doesn't, she sure as heck won't be chasing him; she'd be too busy looking for the next lucky guy to land some of her attention. Which, of course, will make him wonder where he failed. If he has any sense of pride, he's going to up his game, and demonstrate that he is worth pursuing. It is a catch-22, of course. If you chase him, he loses interest. If you don't, he wants you to. Sound familiar? Kind of like that dorky guy who asked you out endlessly, and the more you turned him down, the harder he tried . . . right? Exactly!

Now that you are thinking along those lines, think of what

kinds of boundaries such a girl would maintain:

- What kinds of TMs would be acceptable to her?
- What hours would she consider off-limits?
- What kind of messages is she willing to receive, especially ones of sexual nature? Does this change for her as she gets to know someone better? If yes, at what point do certain things become acceptable?
- What are her rules for accepting a date? Does she accept one via TM? Does this rule change if it is a first date, or if you have been dating for a while?
- What is your policy about last-minute cancellations? Are these deal breakers? If that change is delivered via text, as opposed to phone, does it make a difference?
- What about last-minute plans? Are they acceptable?
- At what point in a relationship—new, early development, or well-developed—are you willing to make exceptions to those rules, once you have established a baseline of respect? Or will you ever accept exceptions?

Keep in mind that when defining your boundaries you want to help him learn to respect your time and your life. This means he will learn to expect that you have plans—even if those plans are to watch reruns of *Friends*, curled up in your pajamas—that cannot necessarily be changed for his convenience, or tardiness in making plans.

What rules or boundaries for text messages from others do you want to set? Consider late night text, text while out with friends, on the job, with family, at events, and booty call text, for starters. What about your feelings on obsessive texts and texts that make you feel bad, or that are sexually overt? How do you feel about these things and what is simply not okay or off-limits for you?

Once you've determined your boundaries, if you find yourself slipping, ask yourself why. Say you suddenly notice you're letting him get away with late night messages, or being textually inappropriate. What gives? Is it simply that you've progressed to a level in your relationship where that makes sense and is something you are comfortable with? Or is it indicative that you are responding to pressure, not wanting to lose him? Knowing your boundaries in advance can help you better analyze your own reasons for letting them slip. At least then you will own the power to recognize what you are doing, and why you are doing it, so you are in a more powerful position from which to determine whether you need to try to curb that behavior. Remember, the first one who has to respect your textual boundaries is you!

Sending Clear Textual Messages

SETTING BOUNDARIES IS ONE THING, but we can't be angry with another for failing to respect those boundaries if we don't send clear messages about what we are willing to accept. Misunderstandings are born when one party neglects to send clear messages about his or her boundaries. If someone seems a bit overtexted, or texts you inappropriately, don't shrug it off. Speaking up is the first step in establishing a boundary. Remember, people will treat us as poorly as we allow them to.

That statement sometimes surprises people. Don't people treat us poorly of their own volition? Well, yes and no. They can, once. The way in which you respond defines the parameters of acceptable behavior. By now you should have gone a long way in defining for yourself the things you are and aren't willing to accept in your life.

Perhaps you feel really strong in your belief that late night booty calls are a no-no. This is probably a wise assessment if your goal is to teach him to respect you and your time, as well as sending out the message that you aren't just waiting around for him. But perhaps the truth is he *is* the guy you want to be with, and you are kind of waiting around for him.

In a nutshell: don't! Fill up your life with exciting activities, so he learns quickly that he had better snag you before you— great catch that you are—slip away.

A great way to drive this home is by assessing the messages you send when you reply to his lame late night textual advances, and they *are* lame if he is just squeezing you in around the rest of his life! Don't you deserve to be the girl who is the center of a guy's world? Of course you do! Hold out for that hero! However, it may be he *is* that hero, but that other women before you have taught him that it is okay to practice some very bad habits. It is up to you to define the boundaries here, by sending clear textual messages that this is not acceptable!

You can tell him outright that you find it disrespectful to expect you to jump at his last-minute efforts. Or you can simply not reply, then let him wonder where you are and who you may be out with! Either acknowledge his text the next day or simply ignore it, demonstrating that you do not respond to such discourteous behavior.

The point is, don't give in. Yes, I know you like him and you want to see him. However, the behavior you accept early in the relationship will set the pace for the entire relationship. Do you want to spend your life constantly anxious, always home because you didn't want to make other plans in case he texted you? No way! Get out there and have a life! If he is meant to be *the one*, then he will quickly step up and act accordingly when he sees you will not accept that kind of behavior. And if not, tell yourself, guess it wasn't him. The universe must hold someone even better! If you don't demonstrate to others that you acknowledge your self-worth, why would they do so? That is what boundaries are really about, demonstrating to him that you are indeed someone worth the effort. And in turn, if he is not someone worthy of showing effort, then he is not the man for you! So don't slip on this. Be clear that you don't tolerate such things.

Now what about Mr. Textually Obsessed, or the guy with the habit of texting you cryptic or confusing messages, or worse yet, the guy who doesn't acknowledge that you are in a situation where it is inappropriate to be carrying on textual communications and he continues to set your pocket vibrating? These are all examples of where you must exercise clarity with precision. You must let him know clearly and directly what the problem is.

You cannot, however, be clear and direct if you don't know for yourself what your rules are for such things. Is it okay to allow the guy who may be *the one* to walk all over you and keep you sitting on edge, or jeopardize your work or school life, just because he doesn't understand appropriate timing or step up to bat? Is it all right for him to throw you into confusion with cryptic messages designed to confuse? Or what about just plain old insensitivity in communication, or the lack thereof? If he keeps you anxious all day long, awaiting a response, how is that affecting your life?

Before you can be clearly textual with him, you have to get

clear with yourself. Far too many of us give up huge pieces of ourselves in the hope that he is Mr. Right. This is why we often suffer such heartbreaks, time and again. We accept bad behavior assuming "he doesn't mean it" when in reality we just aren't ready to accept that maybe, just maybe, he does. We get so blinded by our great white hope that we accept these behaviors and spend our life wondering what *we* did wrong, instead of asking ourselves, why does he behave so poorly?

Again, maybe it isn't his fault; maybe he has fallen into some very bad habits thanks to the women who came before you. However, if that is the case, then you must show him, and quickly, what behavior is acceptable in your world. And in regard to your textual relationship, you have to do this clearly. Finally, in order to do so with clarity, you must first get clear with yourself. What behaviors are you willing to accept in order to be loved? Where can you lower expectations?

- *The endless anxiety of analyzing what he means when it isn't clear if he likes you:* Is this worth it, or is it better to just get involved in your life?
- *Sitting at home, making yourself available in case he texts or calls:* Rather than getting out with friends, or hitting the gym, or taking up a new hobby, is he really worth it, or can you find it in yourself to trust that if he is worth your while he will figure out how to pursue you, and will indeed pursue?
- *Your willingness to give yourself away in a late night booty call*

in a relationship so ambiguous that you have no clue where it is heading: Are you hoping that he may find your accommodating him in the middle of the night a reason to fall in love with you? Or do you want to hold out for someone who knows how to court you respectfully?

- *So desperate for a date that you are willing to keep your calendar clear of time with friends, hobbies, and activities, to accommodate him when he texts you at the last minute:* Are you willing to trust that your own life and experiences are important enough to put first, and that if it is indeed meant to be, he will find a way to get more involved in your world, such as by asking you earlier for that date?

Remember, the treatment you accept now will help define the treatment throughout the relationship, and the little ways in which TM can be used to break down rules of behavior that were once far more respected can truly impact the overall feel of a relationship and define what kind of relationship it will turn out to be. If you want a long-term relationship built on mutual respect, love, and honor, you need to set the tone for all of your communications, and not overlook how little things like the way TM is used between the two of you can shape that.

How will you enforce textual boundaries if they are broken, for example, with too many texts, or texts at inappropriate times?

Are there some rules or boundaries you are okay letting go of in a more established relationship? If so, which ones are they, and at what stage of the relationship is it okay to let that boundary fall away?

▄▄▖▌ Tough Text

THERE ARE TIMES WHEN no matter how politely we try to remind someone of our boundaries, he keeps pushing the limits of acceptable textual behavior. Times like this call for a bit of tough text.

Just like tough love, you must sometimes practice tough text. This means that you have to harden up and stand firm in your boundaries. Remember all those things you analyzed for yourself, all those boundaries you created for your own behavior and what is acceptable from others? Well, while that part took quite a bit of contemplation and consideration on your part, as did letting others know what they are, here comes the place where you get to learn what you're made of. Will you stand up for yourself and honor your own rules of engagement? Because I'll tell you what. If you don't, don't expect anyone else to. It comes right back to: We teach people how to treat us, by letting them see what is or is not acceptable behavior.

So, if you have someone who insists on texting you at inappropriate times, while at work or school, or late at night for booty calls, or in any of the myriad ways that can cross your boundaries, and they don't take the hint no matter how clearly you give it, well then, you are going to have to step up. Yes, I know you don't want to be mean to him, and you certainly don't want to hurt his feelings if you are hoping he is *the one*, but even if he is, you still have to show him how you will and will not be treated. Too often we have the misconception that just because someone is seemingly *the one,* everything he does is going to be right for us. That isn't always true! In fact, you will be doing him a favor if you let him know clearly, up front, what is and is not okay with you.

I'll let you in on another little secret, too. If you do this, you will have a better relationship. How so? Say, for example, that he has a tendency to call you each afternoon at work, and you are starting to suffer some fallout because of it, but you don't want to tell him. You're glad he's calling at all, right? But, as tension builds in your job over this, you will become tenser, and that energy will come across in your interaction with him. Who knows what can come of that? If he gets you on the right day, maybe when you're in the heat of PMS, have a flat, have a run in your stockings, and just got another irritated look from your boss, you may even blow up at him for calling you at work. And the poor guy? He's perplexed. He never knew there was anything wrong to begin with.

People do little things like this all the time. They are afraid to speak up for themselves, don't want to hurt someone's feelings, or offend them, or scare them off, and then we let our boundaries slip more and more until, bam! We get angry and it seems totally out of the blue to the other person, even though for you it may have been building for months on end. Setting boundaries and making them clear can help prevent this and all sorts of other misunderstandings.

Now that you understand this, what if indeed you are honest about your boundaries, and tell a guy, "Hey, this isn't cool, please don't text me at _____, or about _____," and he still does? You have to decide for yourself your policy on this. If he is making a major transgression such as sexually inappropriate language, or middle-of-the-night calls, you may want to take a hard line with him. If he simply seems to have forgotten that you are in yoga class at four p.m. (and please don't text him then either), you may want to cut him some slack the first couple of times he does so, with a gentle reminder of, "Sorry babe, but I'm in yoga from four to five, remember? Bad time to text."

However, for the repeat offender, especially if it is for a more serious matter, you may have to get a bit firmer. Remember, don't feel bad about doing this, or concerned that you may scare the right guy away. The right guy is going to have respect for your guarding your boundaries. If it is someone you really care about and hope to see things progress with, try talking honestly about why you have the boundary, if you'd like.

Explain why it is important to you, and unless he has a good counterargument that you honestly agree with, then you need to explain to him that this is something that is important to you, and that you hope he respects and cares enough for you to understand it, or to support it at the very least. If he can't, then ask yourself this: What else in your life may he be unwilling to understand or support? Will he always dismiss your feelings so easily?

This may sound overreactionary, but you have the opportunity, when setting and maintaining boundaries with something as simple as text messaging, to actually learn a lot about the guy you are dating. You get to learn the levels of respect and understanding he is willing to demonstrate, for instance.

What if, however, the textual obsession grows to become more than just a nuisance? If you have been maintaining your boundaries and giving clear signals that attention is unwanted, and it still persists, take the situation seriously. First, make sure you tell the offensive texter emphatically, "Do not text me again. Your texts and calls are unwelcome." If he contacts you again, you may want to repeat yourself and add, "If you persist, I will have no choice but to take legal action. This is harassment." You may also wish to contact your cell phone provider to have the number blocked. This is for your own safety, but also to save money. If you don't have unlimited texting, those costs can really shoot up!

Next, you may want to consider filing a written report with the police. You should keep a record of the times/dates/content of messages, and record when you asked the text offender to cease and desist.

Don't take stalking lightly; you never know when someone can go over the edge. This is the real world, and bad things happen to great girls every day. Err on the side of caution. This is not the time to feel bad for him. If a man cannot take a direct message to please leave you alone, you cannot know what other impulses he can't resist. Harassment and stalking in TM is as serious and real as it is via other methods. Until the situation is rectified, if you travel alone, do so with great caution.

Your Textual Preference

Another fascinating way to look at TM is as a tool for filtering new relationships to ensure they meet your textual preferences, not only in the textual world, but your relationship preferences in the real world as well.

It is easy for a girl to get carried away when an exciting new guy enters her life. Our hearts go atwitter, and we can fall into the trap of focusing only on his good points, missing all the negatives. We can also err by falling for what he says without looking to see if it matches his actions. If his actions and words aren't in alignment, we are left open to the risk of some serious heartache, and with the advent of modern, highly textual relationships, this is potentially a greater risk than ever before.

Determine if how he interacts with you over TM translates into how he treats you in the real world.

* Does he respect your textual boundaries? Or does he argue and push past them, or dismiss them as silly? If so, make sure this doesn't extend to how he treats you in other areas of your life, too.

* How clear is he in communicating with you? Does he

respond with concern, compassion, and kindness during your communications, textual and otherwise?

* Does he text you back within a reasonable amount of time? Is he clearly making his relationship with you a priority?

* When he is out and about, does he pay attention to you? Or is he too busy texting his buddies instead?

* Is he obsessive and controlling in TM? Is he also controlling in other areas of your life?

* If you talk to him about a concern of yours, such as respecting your boundaries or inappropriate textuality, how does he handle that talk? Is he respectful? Concerned about your feelings?

If you approach your TM interactions with conscious intent, you can see rather quickly whether this guy is a keeper, and if not, you can move on more quickly toward finding the right textual—and perhaps life—partner for you!

◼◼◼◼ Respecting Others' Textuality

Just as we want others to respect our textual boundaries, we must do the same in return. Yes, even when we think they are unreasonable. Just as you will be looking at how he respects your wants, needs, and desires, so too must you respect his.

Yes, maybe it is unfair that he wants you not to text him when he's out with the guys. That is when you probably feel most disconnected from him, and maybe even a bit threatened depending upon the friends he's with, where he's going, and your own relationship histories. However, remember that it is important to build trust. The more you work on that, the more he will respect you, and hopefully the more he will be inspired to step up and become the man you hope him to be. A key element of trust is respect. If he sets a boundary, you must respect it. If you honestly feel strongly about it, discuss it with him at a neutral time (not as he is just about to head out with the guys!). Whatever the boundary, you may feel his reasons are silly and pointless. You may want to argue with them, just as he may feel the same about some of your boundaries. Again, this can serve as a great way to assess how you two can discuss things. Can you do so respectfully? Without attacking one another? Good. If you disagree with his reasons, can you present your argument while honoring him as a person? If so, excellent.

What if you make a really good argument, but he still feels it's something he won't change? You have two choices: You can look at how important it is to you. Is it a deal breaker? Is it indicative of other problems? What is it making you feel? Fear? Jealousy? You may want to look at his deeper emotional reasons. They could be anything. Maybe he is simply afraid of feeling like someone is about to swoop in and take over his life—guys fear things like that! Or maybe he really is a player. You can't know for sure at this stage. You may want to watch for other signals that would indicate it could be either reason. But don't look too hard, or you will obsess it right into reality!

Try extending a little trust and respect here. Okay, his reasons for the boundary make no sense to you. That is where you look at the first option, or move on to the second. You can decide to honor and respect his request no matter how silly you think it is. I'll tell you what. If you do, you will earn his respect in return. This goes a long way in relationship building; extending trust and respect even when you have made a clear argument as to why you aren't comfortable with it demonstrates maturity.

The bottom line is this: He has set a boundary, and if you cannot respect it, you are going to send him major signals that could send off warning bells in his head! By all means, respect his boundaries, just as you'd want others to respect yours.

Chapter 6

Your Guide to Great Text

THROUGHOUT THIS BOOK WE'VE EXAMINED the elements involved in mastering the art of great textual intercourse. You've learned the basics for developing a strong sense of textual confidence, from how to remain safe to basic text-iquette. You are probably feeling far more confident now, and have taken greater command of your text life. However, there are certain nuances that help you go from good to great, and I know you want to have a truly great text life, or you wouldn't be holding this book in your hot little hands. You'd be fondling your cell phone instead!

Diving into the nuts and bolts of great texting will show you the mechanics that create a great text life; however, do not underestimate the importance of the work you did in prior chapters. The steps you took defining the kind of textual inter-course you want to have, and the establishment of textual boundaries, are the framework upon which your entire text life hangs. That framework will shape and mold not only the ways in which you communicate textually, but also many elements of the relationship itself. You see, we oftentimes make the mistake of looking at things piecemeal. For instance, you probably picked up this book thinking it was simply about text messaging within your relationship. However, the key is that text messaging exists within the framework of your relationship itself. These create a system which is a full circuit. The relationship itself will define how you interact in text messages, and the text messages, in turn, will help define your relationship.

How is this so? Quite simply, we have been walking through the process of what a philosopher would call "living the examined life." This means you are examining your intention behind your communications and actions. If you truly want an outstanding text life, you need to create an outstanding relationship. And if you want to have an outstanding relationship, the ways in which you communicate—of which TM is probably a huge part—should be outstanding, too. This is why we have taken such a close look at the framework itself, examining who and how you want to be.

Now that you've determined those things, you can look at different tools with which to deliver your textual communications so that they better meet your intention of who you want to be, and how you shape and mold your relationship. You've done the hardest part. The things you will find in this chapter and beyond will now raise you to the next level. You will discover different delivery mechanisms that sweeten the ways in which your message is received, so that you can bring the results into alignment with the goal you are hoping to achieve.

▂▁█▐ Rhythm and Pacing

Now that you know when you should and shouldn't text, we are going to examine an important nuance for those times it is appropriate to text: rhythm and pacing. Just as a master composer knows that the trick to creating great music rests not only in the arrangement of the notes, but also in the empty spaces between them, so too does the great texter know that there are times when an immediate response is needed, and those when building a little bit of anticipation can go a long way toward building textual tension that is all the more textually satisfying.

As with all elements of texting, if you know your desired outcome, which you should be used to thinking about by now having worked through earlier parts of this book, you can utilize pacing to help create a more fulfilling textual experience.

You could have any number of intended outcomes: to assure; to get his attention; to drive him crazy; even to irritate him if you've got an exceptionally bad case of PMS and he's been acting exceptionally frustrating. If you want to create that final outcome, you probably don't need my help; I'm sure you'll figure out how to push his buttons on your own. But for the rest, let's take a look at ways in which you can utilize rhythm and pacing to enhance your textual intercourse.

TEXTUAL ASSURANCE

If your goal is to assure your partner, to let him know you are indeed on your way and only running late, to soothe his feelings when you've experienced a bump in your relationship, or when you know he's in a situation where he's feeling vulnerable, you will want to be as available as possible via text. Immediacy can be useful here, letting him know you care and are supportive of him. If you take a long time to respond to him, he will quite possibly feel unsupported, wondering what is taking your attention away. Just think about how you would feel if the shoe were on your nicely pedicured foot rather than his. Wouldn't you want that extra bit of attention and a quick response to make you feel more confident in the situation? Of course you would! Well, quite likely, so would he!

COMMANDING HIS TEXTUAL ATTENTION

If your goal is to get his attention, you will want to think along the lines of the fun approaches found in the *Hot Text!* section of this book. Sending off a funny or teasing remark and then getting right back to your day can go a long way in getting his attention.

Remember, there are lots of ways to get his attention, not just sexually. You could send him a quick update on a fascinating news story you just heard about; an update on the score of the game if he's trapped at work and can't watch; or any other piece of information that will serve to remind him, "Wow, what a girl I've got!" However, make sure you are selective here, as elsewhere in your life, and save the attention-getting texts for when you really, truly want attention.

Then again, that assumes you want his *positive* attention. Sometimes a gal actually wants negative attention. She wants him to know she is upset, and she wants him to know it well. An emotionally mature girl will say something like, "We need to get together and talk." That, trust me, will get his attention, although be forewarned: many guys will insist you talk right then and there. The last thing I would advise is for you to have any kind of important discussion via text. If you are not feeling the urgency to spill your heart in the moment to the point where you must resort to text, then why not just schedule a date to get together and talk in person?

Unfortunately, there are times when many of us simply feel it cannot wait. We can be highly emotional creatures with hugely loving hearts. If you feel you must throw a tantrum here and now, remember there are consequences. You will likely get his attention quite successfully, and maybe even his compassion. However, you may want to stop and ask yourself: Are those the ways in which you want to get his attention? Wouldn't you feel more satisfied getting it for being wonderful, fantastic you, than for having thrown a fit? Remember, eyes on the prize. You want the guy, but you want him in a highly respectful way that honors both of you. Don't you?

DRIVING HIM WILD

If your goal is to drive him wild, pacing and rhythm can certainly contribute. Again, being suggestive rather than overt is key. It can charge him up faster than your little iPhone could ever get juiced up! This is especially true if you reserve such texts for random occasions. Remember, less can be more. If he is used to getting such messages from you, they are no longer likely to be attention getters. That is the biggest key to using rhythm and pacing to drive him wild; use it selectively, and let him learn that when you set this pattern of TM in motion, he is in for some pleasant surprises.

▪▫▪◼ *Clearly Textual*

THERE ARE TIMES WHEN a cryptic message can be alluring, but normally something unclear is more confusing than anything else. If your intention is to be truly great at text, you must master the art of saying what you mean, and meaning what you say, in as few words as possible. You must find a way to fill in for all the missing pieces, such as tonality, expression, and inflection, and all in the space of a few characters! Master that, and you truly deserve the title of Textual Expert. Let's take a look at some ways in which to do this.

EXPRESS YOUR MOOD OR INTENT

In the hope of avoiding misunderstandings, you will want to let the recipient of your message know the context in which you are delivering. Is it intended to be funny or serious? Are you being sarcastic? Making an effort to include cues as to your intended delivery can go a long way in creating clarity.

One way to help the other party to sense the mood or intention of your TM is to utilize descriptive adjectives. Another is to use mood-describing abbreviations. A basic example of this would be "LOL," shorthand for "laughing out loud," if you find something funny. Utilizing abbreviations can help you say a lot more in your TM and can serve as helpful cues.

Another way to cue your textual partner in on the spirit of

the message is to use emoticons. A smiley face or wink can go a long way in helping to define the intended meaning of the message. See page 169 for a list of useful emoticons.

CHEAP TEXT

Be a cheap texter! By this I mean, if you can say it with less, all the better. Utilizing text abbreviations will help you say a lot more, with far less text. Again, as with the use of "LOL," these deliver a better sense of your meaning, while cutting down on the amount of space it takes to do so. There are literally hundreds of common text abbreviations, and as you get to know someone you will come to better "speak one another's language." However, when you are getting to know someone, make sure that you both have the same understanding as to what an abbreviation means! You may even want to discuss it beforehand. See page 170 for a text abbreviation dictionary that can help you find some great shortcuts.

TEXTUAL CLARITY

Finally, rather than focusing on using an impressive vocabulary, seek words that clearly, simply, and most accurately communicate what you are trying to say. Remember, TM tends to happen at a rapid pace, and often people read their TMs while doing other things. So try to be as brief, specific, and to the point as possible, choosing the simplest, most straightforward words to deliver your message. Just follow this adage: Say what you mean, and mean what you say, and do it as directly as possible.

Remember, textual clarity helps prevent misunderstandings and creates good, strong communication. It is worth the extra effort to ensure your messages are being received as clearly as possible. The few seconds of time you invest in considering this can go a long way toward creating harmonious communications.

Textual Humor

INJECTING A BIT OF HUMOR into your text life can go a long way toward making your texts extra special. This is no easy feat when you consider how few characters you have at your disposal. However, with a little bit of thought, you can definitely rack up a few laughs along with your cell phone bill. This is something to be approached carefully. You never know how the party on the other end will interpret it. You could say something like, "Oh yeah, real cute!" and the other party will be left wondering if you mean it literally or if you are being sarcastic, thus taking it as an insult you didn't necessarily mean to deliver. If you have any doubt as to whether the person on the other side is going to "get it," you would be wise to err on the side of caution, if you want to avoid textual confusion.

However, if you are in a developed relationship, you probably already have a few running jokes, and referencing them in TM could be a fun way to add levity to your day. You may even want to consider adapting something humorous from your everyday life specifically to create humor in your text messages. The idea is to pick something and utilize it as your humor touchstone, something you can always throw out there for a smile, kind of like a term of endearment, but an amusing one. The benefit of bringing a grin or laugh to your partner's face is that he will come to associate you with someone who makes him feel good, even at random times throughout his day. Never a bad thing!

What Are Your Partner's Textual Needs?

BEFORE YOU SEND OFF THAT WITTY REMARK, pause for a moment and carefully assess the message you are responding to. What do you think your textual partner was looking for? A real answer, or just support, or merely some good vibrations? An important element of great textual intercourse is to try to gauge what your partner really wants; over time he will give plenty of cues. Learn how to fulfill your partner's textual needs.

You would think this is obvious, right? That's not always the case. Just as you oftentimes have an obvious meaning and a deeper *hopeful* meaning to what you write, others can be looking for something very different than what it seems on the outset. Some examples are:

VENTING

Sometimes people just want to vent. They need to express themselves in order to clear their heads. Men are often that way. Many, many men like to solve problems on their own. Sometimes when they tell us a problem they are facing, they aren't really looking for an answer so much as wanting to blow off steam, and are hoping we can just be there as a sounding board. Yes, of course this can lead to misunderstandings, but this is why you should try to filter the situation to get an idea of what your partner is really seeking.

For example, if he is writing you to complain about his boss, this may well be one of those times when he just wants to vent. If you're uncertain, you can ask him outright: "I know that's frustrating. Do you just need to blow off steam, or are you looking for solutions?" Or conversely, you can say, "Have you thought of how you can handle it? I'm here if you want some suggestions, or just someone to listen." In these ways you leave the door open for either support.

FEELING USEFUL

Sometimes a guy will text us almost too much, even when he knows we are out and about or involved in something. It may simply be that he is looking to feel useful. Men tend to like a feeling of accomplishment, of being needed. Is that really so different from us? We need to feel needed, too, don't we? Everyone likes to feel they can make a valuable contribution to the lives of those they care about. Sometimes an overzealous texter may simply be trying to demonstrate that he is there to care and nurture you. If he seems to be doing just that, why not thank him for always providing excellent suggestions and caring to see that you are okay? If you think about it, this is really thoughtful. Please note: If the texter seems to be a dangerous type, or overly obsessed, please consider the steps of action in the *Textual Obsession* section for your safety.

▂▃▅ Textual Interpretation

ANOTHER IMPORTANT ELEMENT OF great text is your own interpretation of your partner's messages, both content and elements such as rhythm and pacing. Just as you are contemplating your own rhythm and pacing, and different elements of your life come into play with it, so it is with him.

Now we all know men can be incredibly cryptic. We have all

known someone who has struggled with trying to figure out what he means, or what the timing of his return call indicates. The same is true in TM, and with TM there are all sorts of additional factors to consider! Where is a girl to begin in assessing his textual intentions?

Good question. Let's take a look at some of the factors you and your friends may endlessly contemplate:

TIMING

Okay, you sent your response three hours ago and haven't heard back from him yet. What gives? He carries his cell everywhere he goes. What does it take, two minutes at most to answer a text? Is he mad? Did he misunderstand what you said? Did he take it the wrong way? Oh no, did you sound dumb? Oh, maybe he doesn't really like you after all! Soon you are going over all your recent interactions, in TM and in person. You may even call on some of your girlfriends to help you analyze this better, because this is serious stuff, right? Actually, come to think of it, maybe you should resend the text, in case it didn't get to him somehow.

Oh no you don't! Take a deep breath and put down that cell. Yes! Step away from the cell, right now. This is where you risk crossing over into an obsessive texter, going from being the *it girl* to *that girl*! Stop analyzing. Stop and think: Maybe he is just busy. Maybe he is so certain of your feelings for him and your overall capability that he figures he can get back to you later.

Don't make the mistake of assuming his delayed response is due to lack of interest; he may legitimately be busy. Or he may even be out of range, or maybe his battery died. Unless you had plans he isn't showing up for, do not assume the worst.

If, however, he doesn't get back to you eventually, you may want to cool your heels a bit and let him get back to pursuing you for a while. Busy your schedule up. Usually that will bring him around quickly, as he wonders what he was doing wrong or who has been keeping you occupied. Try not to analyze too much the length of time between his messages, unless it is clear to you that you're playing a little bit of a romantic cat and mouse game, intended to lead up to some steamy fun later on.

WHEN YOU JUST DON'T "GET" HIS MESSAGES

Sometimes no matter how smart he is, or how much you like or love him, a guy can send a TM that just doesn't seem to make sense to you. You sit there rereading it again and again, trying to assess the meaning. Instead of driving yourself nuts, ask for clarification! It will be far worse if you guess at his meaning, and guess wrong. If you don't understand, or if you question whether it was a joke or serious, definitely ask. Far too often a girl will read too much into a message a guy just quickly shot off, and feel either sad or exhilarated for all the wrong reasons. Try to take his messages at face value; guys rarely put as much focus into little quickie text messages as we ladies tend to. Unless you have reason to believe otherwise, assume the message means pretty much what it says.

Chapter 7

Hot Text!

NOW THAT YOU'VE EXPLORED the many ways in which to engage text messaging to create a healthy, successful relationship, and explored the dos and don'ts of good text-iquette, what about utilizing it to literally cause a little stimulation? As you are probably well aware, text messaging has become a new avenue for erotica, yet another way in which to tease and tantalize your partner, bringing phone sex and good vibrations to a whole new level.

If you decide you would like to utilize TM to spice up your romance, you will be joining the ranks of many millions of people who find this a fun and inviting way to add another dimension to their relationships. As with everything else we've examined, you must begin by defining your aim. People explore erotic TM for many reasons and you must determine what yours is. There are as many reasons as there are types of relationships. Some of the reasons people engage in steamy text include: looking to add a little spice to their relationship; to tease their partner just enough to keep themselves foremost in his mind; as foreplay to an encounter to be had later in the day; just for fun; to stay sexually connected when separated by distance or circumstance; to explore things you may be interested in but want to feel out your partner's response to. All of these are valid reasons.

However, some people engage in erotic TMs for less than healthy reasons, such as an addiction to sex, or because they are afraid if they don't their partner will stray. If you find yourself creating textual stimulation for these reasons, you may want to assess the situation and talk with your partner about your fears or concerns, and if appropriate, seek outside help.

But if you are considering textual stimulation for all the right reasons, you may want to try some of the suggestions in this chapter to help stroke your partner's textual desire. As with all methods of seduction, there is an art to it. Granted, anyone can dash off graphic messages. That doesn't make them truly hot, though. Why not? Simply because *anyone* can do that. Do you want to be just anyone to him? Of course not! You want to be his hottest textual experience? Of course you do. That takes a more serious kind of stimulation, one that involves his mind on a deeper, more engaged level. Well then, let's look at ways in which to raise the textual temperature to the max with some of the tantalizing teasery below.

Text and Deny

SENDING A TEASING, TEMPTING MESSAGE and then being unavailable can build tension. It will definitely keep you on his mind. I'm not saying play cruel mind games, but it comes back to pacing. Making him wait a little bit longer for a response reminds him you have a life too. He will be fascinated (and maybe a little bit concerned) by what could possibly have been more intriguing than responding to his text.

Think of this as an innocent game of cat and mouse. Engage in this guiltless teasery at a time when he knows you are likely busy and unable to get back to him right away, so he has no reason to feel rejected even momentarily. Perhaps while working or at an event you couldn't get out of even though you'd rather be back home with him, you can sneak off and send a quick hot text telling him something that could have a double meaning, something indirectly teasing and tantalizing. Perhaps you could text that you just ducked out to freshen up and decided to drop him a line, but you have to go back out to perform your big presentation . . . while dropping a hint that you'd rather be performing on *him* right now. . . . Any kind of little lead-in that says, *I want to be with you right now,* in a naughty kind of way, but in a way that is a tiny bit elusive. Or you could make a reference to a particularly hot time you shared in the past: "Wow, it's hot out here today. I haven't felt this hot since that night in Cancun with you." You may also want to try, "Can't wait to seduce you tonight" or, "Later tonight, I'll tell you all the fantasies that drive me wild . . ." before getting back to your day.

Anyone can shoot off something graphic, but you want his mind to travel to things that link his steamy thoughts directly to you and times you have spent together, or times you will spend together soon. Dropping hints, then taking off for a bit, giving some time before responding to his comeback—can heat up a lot more than your overworked little cell phone. Do this, and you become not just someone sending him taunting messages, but messages that specifically link him to past, present, and future times together, personally tailored to his tastes, or which are allowing his own naughty fantasy to fill in with his own version of pleasure involving you.

This is something that someone using just the repertoire of plain old graphic "same old same old" cannot begin to offer. So use a bit of teasery, get his mind going, and then get back to being busy with your life for a bit. Let his mind take that time to fill in all the blanks, and to wrap itself more around the idea of the two of you together. When you respond again, offer just another glimpse of teasing pleasure, but don't promise a time for fulfillment. Don't say you won't see him soon, but play this moment a bit coy, not because you want to play games with him, but because you want to raise his passion to the peak. It will most definitely keep you on his mind. Just wait until he sees you again!

▄▄▆█ Text U Up 2-Nite

THROUGHOUT THE DAY, YOU AND YOUR PARTNER can play a game, texting what you want to do tonight, but again, make it more challenging by trying to keep the word choice clean. It will encourage you to create a language of your own, your own little textual messages that no one else can understand. Finding creative ways to describe how you will ravish each other when together again will bond you more deeply. Plus, there is an added advantage that someone else glancing at the message coming in will be less likely to understand what you are referring to!

I know one couple who talks of everything in terms of pastry delicacies. Their playful text talk describes how hot they are going to get later on, when they are cooking, and if you cut through the double entendre of sugary goodness and hot and hearty baking designed to get a rise out of each other, you will see that not only is this a sexy, teasing way to entertain a bit of foreplay, but it is also incredibly fun!

However, even if you would prefer to use straightforward language, the point here is, you can use this time to stretch your foreplay out for hours on end. It is a bit different from using text and deny, because this is a steadier, direct stream of conversation, though you could certainly mix the two, as well.

Why not come up with some creative starters for yourself so that you have them on hand next time you want to explore this option?

Textual Exploration

BY MUTUAL AGREEMENT, you and your partner can text each other fantasies you may not feel quite as comfortable sharing in person. You may want to create an agreement that you won't judge or accuse each other; what happens in text-land, stays in text-land (unless you agree to try it out in the real world). You can even text through the experience itself, living the fantasy out virtually, to try it on and see how you may feel.

The semi-anonymity of discussing one's fantasies in TM rather than in person can go a long way toward helping someone shy get past his or her fears of discussing secret fantasies, especially if it is agreed upon that you don't necessarily have to act upon them in real life.

Sometimes just initiating such a conversation in a safe-feeling arena such as TM allows you to talk about it openly in person, too. The idea here is that the world of TM can create a neutral playground upon which you can initiate what would otherwise seem like risqué or even emotionally frightening fantasies you want to share.

This can be as innocent or as raunchy as you like, and it is applicable to the casual relationship as much as it is to the long-term one. Again, it depends on what your aim is. Are you sharing the fantasy because you want to actually try it out? Or to gauge your partner's response to the idea of it? Or just to enjoy the indulgence of daydreaming about it? Any and all of these are fine, so long as your partner is comfortable with it too.

Remember, before you proceed, ensure that you aren't violating your partner's textual boundaries with such material. In order for this to work well, everyone has to feel safe and respected. Creating that safe space can go a long way toward opening up new doors of potentiality, as well as new avenues of communication, all of which can help build a stronger relationship, both textually and otherwise.

▂▃▅ Role-Text

SOME PEOPLE ENJOY ROLE-PLAYING as a way to charge up their sex lives, exploring what it is like to step inside someone else's shoes for just a little while. It doesn't have to be just a naughty game. You can do the same with texting, exploring a wide variety of personalities and scenarios. In the same way in which you may want to try out new fantasies in TM, you can also play around with a different persona. Perhaps you want to try to be a little more assertive. What better way to try on a new attitude than in TM, where you have the opportunity to take it for a "text drive"? If it doesn't go over well you can simply apologize with, "Sorry it came across that way. You know how TM can be."

Whether you want to try out a new attitude or a new joke, TM could be a fun place to try it on for size. If you know you have a relatively safe arena, you may find you can explore far more personal growth than you might otherwise have had the courage to attempt.

In the end, that new attitude or shift in confidence could be incredibly sexy on you, or totally inspire a new phase of interest in your life that spills over into all that you do, including steaming up your text life.

Chapter 8

Textual Healing

WHEN YOUR RELATIONSHIP HITS A RUT, you may well find that you can create a little bit of textual healing. Perhaps your loved one is feeling neglected? Maybe you've taken him a little too much for granted? Or perhaps you've been a bit overly textual with him? No worries; that little powerhouse of a cell phone can help you make amends. Granted, nothing takes the place of an in-person apology that includes your taking accountability for your wrongdoing, demonstrating that you own the error of your ways and are not making excuses for those mistakes. That is an important element of integrity in a relationship, both to you and to the other party, and must be handled properly in order for healing to begin. However, once you have addressed the issue at hand, you can utilize that sleek little baby in your hot hands to begin righting those wrongs more directly. This chapter will show you how.

...ıll Textual Connection

When you've hurt or wronged your partner, or haven't given him the attention or props he deserves, your cell phone can be a great tool to help you reconnect as you are making amends. If you are guilty of neglect, or of taking him for granted, make sure you give him a little bit of textual attention, expressing your affection. Open yourself up textually; make yourself available, or drop a well-timed message of support or encouragement. Even just an "I love you" can go a long way toward healing some hurt.

If the problem is that you get caught up in your day, or just plain have an awful memory, you hold in your hands another key to addressing that: your reminder system. Set a reminder for yourself to drop a quick but affectionate text, letting him know you are thinking of him. Don't let him know you've had to put in a reminder to do so; that will detract from the process. In fact, don't even enter the reminder under his name. Create a code for yourself, lest he catch on. Furthermore, don't do it at the same time each day. He may catch on and feel more hurt that you had to remind yourself to think of him.

Just think of how it would feel were you the one being neglected. And think of the things you would want to hear, or that would make you feel appreciated. People love to feel appreciated, and a message that acknowledges how patient he is with you, or how grateful you are for the little things he does (be specific!), can go a long way toward making him feel great. The more we know our efforts are appreciated, the more we are likely to repeat them.

Maybe your case is different, though. Maybe he is just upset that you've left him behind as you go off with the girls, or on a weekend getaway. First of all, kudos to you! Great way to let him see how exciting your life is, and that you are focused on filling it with wonderful, fulfilling activities. However, you will want to soothe his concerns a bit by dropping him a line while away to let him know he's in your thoughts. Not too much, though. You want him to realize you can indeed be happy without him, which will make him feel the need to demonstrate all the more how valuable an asset he is to your life. However, you don't want to crush the poor guy either. If (and only if) he has expressed hurt or concern, you can create a lot of healing with a couple of well-placed TMs letting him know he isn't forgotten. Again, if you're concerned you'll get too caught up in the moment to remember to do so, set a reminder, or if your cell phone allows you to set up automated TMs, do so before you leave.

If the problem is the inverse, that you have been overly textual with him, then it is time to step back. Go back to the beginning of this book and reread the section on *Textual Preference*. Who do you want to be? What part of yourself do you want to reveal? Are you truly a girl who lets her emotions drive her amuck, or do you possess the power of reason? Can you step back and see the big picture, and the ways in which caving in to instant gratification can actually rob you of the greater prize in the grand scheme of things? Can you see how surrendering to the baser drives can cost you what you want most, working against you even as you are trying to get closer?

Okay . . . you get it . . . but you still can't help it. If you don't know how to resist the impulse to text him, try giving yourself something else to do. Like ten sit-ups (think how flat your belly will be if you do that every time you feel driven to text him—wow!). Or opening the dictionary to learn a new word (no, you cannot text him about the great new word you learned!). The one thing I would NOT suggest is texting your friends about the desire to text him. Once you have those out-of-control fingers on your keypad, you might just cave.

There is also another approach. You can try a visualization method. Go to a quiet space and close your eyes. Take several long, slow inhalations, followed by long, slow exhalations. Picture yourself texting him. Really get the image clear. See the phone in your hands. Feel its weight. Feel the pressure of your fingers against the keypad as you begin to text. Sense the rush of excitement when you hit *send*.

Now get him in your mind. Picture him in all his loving wonder. See him opening up his phone, looking down at your

TM and turning to his buddy saying, "Oh man, it's *her* again," before hitting *delete*. Picture him talking with his buddies about how neurotic you are, and how he's getting tired of hearing from you all the time. Remember how bad you felt the last time you two had an argument about your obsessive textiness. Remember the look on his face. Feel the image of him receiving the message growing bigger and bigger, until it replaces the one of you sending the message. Repeat this several times, and you will begin to replace your positive neural associations of sending TMs with negative ones.

If that isn't enough to scare you out of your overtextual tendencies, you may need to seek outside help! Seriously, though, remember that text can be used for good or bad. You can allow it to become a tool for healing and becoming deeply connected, or you can turn it into something that comes between you. I suggest you use your cellular power for good!

Help for the Overtexted

If the problem is that you've been overly texty, bordering on clingy and obsessive, you can still create some textual healing. You must learn to tame your texting habits. Yes, there are a million things you want to say to him, but you are going to have to be selective as to what you text him. Besides, don't you want something exciting left to share with him when you see him again? If you share everything with him throughout the day, what are you going to talk about when you get together?

If you keep your eyes on the prize and your bigger goals for interacting with him (to create a fantastic, fulfilling relationship), you will realize that your momentary drive to text him can undo exactly that which you are working toward. Self-control is the key here. You don't want to undo the makings of a good relationship by overwhelming him, and far too many men tell tales of being scared away by a partner's overindulgent textual habits. So let's heal some of that textual drama before it's too late. Let's look at ways in which to do so:

TEXTUAL INTENTION

He accuses you of overtexting. Instead of just focusing on quitting cold turkey, let's try examining the root cause of the problem; let's look at the intentions behind your texting him. Are you feeling needy, clingy, or insecure? Are you texting for validation? Are you simply bored? Or just excited at the prospect of sharing your day with him? Or are you forwarding vital information whose importance he doesn't understand? If you aren't making things clear, and your texts are interpreted as trivial, he may feel that you are interrupting his day with little things you can share later. Clarity is important; check with yourself on your intention for sending the TM. Are you really sending it because you are feeling lonely or insecure? Don't forget that a world existed long before TM, and even longer before e-mail and cell phones. Once upon a time, for many generations in fact, relationships survived just fine, even without instant communication. If your partner is feeling overwhelmed, check your intention and ask yourself, can this wait until I see him? Just asking yourself the question may help you cut back on the habit.

THE THREE-MINUTE RULE

If you need to cleanse your relationship of overtextualization, you may want to begin applying the three-minute rule. Whenever you feel tempted to send off a TM, stop and pause for three minutes before doing so. At this time, you may want to check in with yourself about intention, or even just go for a walk, call up a friend, or change your activity of the moment. This may be enough to get you through the urge to shower him with your textual attention.

WRITTEN TEXT

If you really have trouble overcoming your textual urges, try keeping a notebook handy and writing down all the things you wanted to text him during the day. As you come to day's end, you can review the list and ask yourself: How important were these things? Were any of them important enough to cause the stress in this relationship that the arguing over my rate of texting was causing? If you practice this for a few weeks, you will come to see patterns emerge, and be able to better clarify which TMs should be sent, and which information can be saved till later. I'm sure that having less stress in your relationship overall will reinforce for you the feeling that hyper-textuality just isn't worth the damage it does when the other party isn't as enthralled with it as you are.

DE-TEXTIFYING BUDDY

If TM in your relationship is causing undue stress and arguments, and none of the other strategies have worked, why not see if one of your friends would be willing to be your de-textifying buddy? You could text them instead of him, every time you have the urge to text. This way, you can at least get the drive to TM out of your system.

Chapter 9

Textual Dysfunction

YES, YOU LOVE THE PLEASURES OF the textual world. It is stimulating and exciting; it creates the feeling that you are developing close relationships. However, you may have noticed that some of the relationships in your life aren't going so well. Perhaps you've even wound up in textual battlefields, firing off message-bombs that seem like a war of the text-es. Worse still, some of those you feel you give tons of textual attention to, complain that they feel neglected! Or maybe you are just mired in a serious bout of textual confusion. How can that be?

Yes, indeed, that can be a true side effect of the textual wonders you experience. This is where you tumble from being in a healthy textual relationship straight into the dreaded textual dysfunction. You see, textual relationships can be deceiving. You can be led to believe that you are developing strong bonds, when in reality, you can finger your keypad all day long, but never share a true intimacy. You must not fall into the trap of developing textually based relationships. While these can be momentarily exciting, they do not make long-term bonds.

Does that advice seem confusing in a book on textual intercourse? It need not be. While indeed TM can be used to enhance a relationship, it can also undermine it, as you've already seen in some chapters. Additionally, if you find yourself on TM all day long, you could feel you are pretty close to your textual partner; however, quantity does not equal quality. What are you talking about? Are you truly connecting, in the sense of communicating, or simply sending banal text back and forth all day long? Are you discussing things that bring you closer, developing a deeper intimacy in the process? If so, great! If not, you need to go back to the topics at the beginning of this book and ask yourself who you want to be in your relationship, and subsequently who you want to be textually, with your partner.

It is my hope that you learn to utilize TM to create a more deeply connected, bonded relationship that is healthy in every way. In this chapter we will look at textual dysfunction, so you can recognize it if it does begin to sneak in, and so you will know how to address it. We will be looking not only at the emotional elements of textual dysfunction in a relationship, but also at the physical, such as repetitive stress injury, one of the pitfalls of overtexting!

Since we know it isn't likely that a girl like you would fall into such devastating textual dysfunctionality, we will instead focus primarily on what to do when he does. Let us learn what textual dysfunction is, so that we can make sure it never creeps into your life!

▁▂▃▅ Textual Impotence

Perhaps your relationship is going well; the love of your life fails you in only one area—the textual. Try as you may, he never seems to participate actively in your text life; he seems distant or actually avoidant. He even seems to make up excuses to avoid serious textual activity. You see strength in every other area of your relationship. No matter how hard you work at arousing his textual interest, your partner fails to rise to the occasion. You are happy overall, but sometimes you wonder if you'll have to spend the rest of your days living a lackluster text life.

Feeling the warm afterglow of a wonderful evening with him, you eagerly text him the next day, only to get a short, almost terse response, if any at all. Oh no! What could this mean? Maybe it wasn't such a wonderful evening for him? Oh, how the mind starts running through the possibilities! What is going on? And why are you obsessing over it?

In a little while he calls you, and you definitely get the feeling that all is good in the world. So what's the deal with the textual inadequacy? And why *does* it bother you so much?

ASSESS THE SITUATION

Before feeling textually rejected or jumping to the conclusion that he may not be interested, consider other possible causes. Could it be that he doesn't see the things discussed in TM as important? He may just not view TM as a serious means of communication.

On the other hand, it could be that he is simply too busy or distracted through the day, with work, school, and life in general, to be overly involved in textual communications. Or he may be of the ilk that sees TM as a bit silly.

DOES IT MATTER?

Now you need to ask yourself an all-important question: Does it really matter if he's not that into TM? Yes, you were already wondering why it bothered you, right? If you think the problem is indicative that he isn't taking the relationship seriously, then perhaps you need to assess the other areas of your relationship. However, if he demonstrates his devotion in other areas of your life, it may simply be one of the reasons above. If that is a problem to you, if you really need a textually active relationship, then you need to further assess your motives.

How important is it to you to create a text life, and more significantly, why is it important to you? If you're feeling the pain of your partner's textual dysfunctionality, or more accurately, his textual deficiency, then you need to know why. Do you just need more attention throughout the day? A way to feel more connected? Is it simply habitual? Is this what you always did in relationships?

If those are your reasons, you may find a compromise that could work. You could talk with your partner about your need to feel connected throughout the day. You can make this a light, playful talk, such as a teasingly delivered, "Hey, a girl likes a little attention throughout the day to keep her heart aflutter" or "her engine revving" or whatever you want to say. If he doesn't take the hint, and it is really important to you, you can try having a serious talk about it. However, if texting really isn't his thing, you may have to resort to other methods, such as phone calls or e-mails. Remember: What are your intentions? Is it just to get your way, in this case, more TMs from him? Or is it to keep communication going when you are apart? If you figure out what your intention is, then you may be able to find a textually satisfying solution to the situation, if you focus on the true goal of the quality rather than quantity of the textual attention.

If, on the other hand, you realize it may be bothering you because you are feeling it could represent a deeper problem in the relationship, then you need to begin assessing other areas. If you feel his lack of TM response is disrespectful to you, for instance, it may be that you have begun to subconsciously notice that in other areas of the relationship, too. If you consider this a yellow or red flag, it is wise to assess the relationship as a whole, and ask yourself what the lack of textual response represents to you. One of the best ways to handle all of this is to observe, and then to discuss it with your partner.

TEXTUAL CONSIDERATIONS

You may also want to consider the kinds of TMs you send him. Is there one type he responds to more than others? Is he a "strictly business" kind of responder, getting back to you only on things that have a high level of relevance? If so, think of building on strengths here. If you have success with informational texts, for instance, try focusing on building that up. Don't overkill here, but focus on texting only informational updates such as "running late" or "I made the reservations like you asked" rather than gossipy ones. If he begins to grow accustomed to seeing TM with you as practical and useful, you may be able to slowly transition him into other areas of textual intercourse, if you feel you really need more. Again, as with anything else, you may want to sit down and have an open conversation with him about it, asking him if he just feels uncomfortable texting, or is too busy, or whether something else altogether is going on.

Remember, TM should be enhancing your relationship. If it is causing stress, you need to determine what the root cause is, and aim to fix it. If you feel seriously bad about what you perceive as textual dysfunction on his part, again, ask yourself what you really need: A good relationship is not worth throwing away over a lackluster text life. There is far more to relationships than text alone! But, if you are feeling really upset, it may be indicative that there is something else bothering you that may be far more serious in nature, and it would benefit you both to explore what that may be. Either way, don't let someone's lackluster text drive run a relationship into the ground. Good guys are hard to find; if you've found one, teach him how to be more textually active, make it exciting and fun for him, and if that doesn't work, well, let him know you love him either way, and that for you it is about far more than just great text.

▪▫▌▌ Textual Confusion

You know he said it in text, but when you're together in the real world, he just doesn't seem to act the way he did in his messages. What's going on here? It could be any number of problems. But don't panic yet. Take some time to assess the relationship overall, and perhaps the picture will come more clearly into focus. I know textual confusion can be frustrating, but let's walk through it and see what we can figure out before you go jumping to conclusions, okay?

CONTEXTUAL DIFFERENCES

People can have a conversation in which they think they are saying exactly the same thing, only to learn later that they meant something completely opposite. All of this is built with words. When you operate within the textual world, that entire aspect of the relationship is developed around words and what they mean to the two parties holding the conversation. Context is very important, as words have different meanings to different people. So don't be surprised if there is some confusion; it really is natural. Even the strongest couple can experience miscommunication and misunderstanding.

For instance, a message may be intended humorously but, missing the irony, you get insulted—or cause the other person to be insulted. Interpretation must be based on context. If this is the reason for your textual confusion, you may simply need to learn each other's "language" better in order to avoid this, as well as increasing the use of emoticons to help indicate the intended spirit of the message. Emoticons can be found on page 169.

Additionally, in time you will come to learn each other's language patterns. For example, you should eventually learn to better recognize his patterns of sarcasm. Until you master that, when you read his TM, try to hear it in his voice, the way he would say it aloud; that may help you get a better contextual understanding.

ROSE-COLORED TEXT

Unfortunately, sometimes textual confusion is born of someone's reading text messages through the rose-colored glasses of love's great hope. A danger of the textual world is that we can choose to interpret a message in many different ways, and that interpretation grows potentially wider when things like tonality, expression, and body language aren't present. You already saw how the same phrases can be seen in different contexts. Think how much this is exacerbated when you are *hoping* he means something. If you are looking hard enough for meaning in something, you can likely make a good case for claiming you see it there, even when it isn't there at all.

Sometimes that confusion can even come not from his words, but just the amount of textual attention he is giving you. If a guy is texting you all day long, it is easy to believe he is deeply invested in you. So you then get confused when he doesn't seem as serious when you are together, or perhaps doesn't act as a boyfriend would. Unfortunately, just because a guy texts you up all day long doesn't necessarily mean he's in love. It could mean that, but it could also mean he's bored, or sexually and textually infatuated. So, while it may mean your hopes about love are true, it may not. I suggest you step back and take a look at all his actions, in the real and textual world alike.

If you feel unsure about what he means, rather than driving yourself crazy trying to figure it out, or spending hours endlessly analyzing it with your girlfriends, try asking, "What do you mean when you say this?" or saying, "I don't want to read more into this than is here. Maybe we should talk about it." Scary? You bet it is. But is it really scarier than all those hours of anxiously sitting there wondering and analyzing? You don't have to ask it in a high-pressured way. In fact, the more casually you ask it, the better, because he will think you don't care one way or another what he means by it. If he is indeed serious, he will step up and make sure you know it, rather than risk letting you get away. If his intentions are less than what you thought, either you will learn the truth, or your very behavior may make him pause to think, "Hey, why isn't she chasing me down like other girls? She must have something goin' on! I had better take a closer look at this one."

TEXTUAL INSECURITY

There may be an even simpler, absolutely adorable yet frustrating reason as to why your man's words and actions in TM aren't meeting those in the physical world: He may be too shy to say certain things to you face-to-face!

Seriously, there are people who have been known to become dependent upon relating through a slightly more anonymous method such as e-mail or texting. It may be that he lacks confidence in real life, but experiences a tremendous rise in confidence level within the textual world. There he feels safer expressing himself, so he will go further, and then when you are together in person, it feels as though he is holding back. If you sense this is true, you may want to ask, and you may want to cut him a break and ask via text!

Okay, the bottom line is this: If his words aren't meeting his actions, you need to see it as a yellow flag. This doesn't mean throw a fit about it, but it does mean it is time to pause and examine the situation, and your own intentions and expectations. Ask yourself: Is it him, or is it my own expectations? Is he just afraid or not quite that serious? And, if you think it may just be a lack of clarity and understanding, ask him! Asking can be the fastest way out of the land of textual confusion.

...ıll *Textual Fixation*

Many people these days seem to fall into the sketchy land of textual fixation. I'm not talking in this instance of the stalker-ish texter that we've discussed in other areas of this book. No, now I'm going to address the person who is so obsessed with texting that he or she seems to have a cell phone permanently implanted in the hand. They may be texting you when away from you, but when with you, they are constantly texting someone else. It doesn't matter where you are—at a restaurant, a show, in bed—they are ever listening for the tone to announce they have a TM arriving. And let's hope it is your partner who is guilty of this, and not you! If it's you, my dear, you must do what is necessary to break this terrible habit immediately!

The BlackBerry has come to be nicknamed the "CrackBerry" for its highly addictive nature. If you or your partner is living more in the textual world than in the physical one, it is time to look closely at the situation. Your goal is to allow this medium to bring you closer together, but not at the expense of the world around you. Even in the best of relationships, obsession is unhealthy. You must pay attention to those you are with in the moment. Stay focused on the now. Yes, you can briefly TM him to stay connected, but do not fail to value the gift of the moment you are in while focusing on another.

If you find yourself texting during meetings, while eating out with friends, or obsessively in any situation, you need to take a step back and look at your habits. This is the time to revisit the "what is your intention behind the textual attention" concept. When you are focused on texting with a specific intent, you will never text to the exclusion of what is going on in the real world around you; everything will have a place of balance in your life.

If it is your partner who has a textually obsessive personality, use your boundaries to curb his texting, and if he is texting others while out with you, talk with him about it and let him know it makes you feel neglected. If he is that out of control in his textual habits, you will need to make it clear that if he would rather be lost in the world of textuality instead of interacting with you, you can head on home and give him all the space he needs. Seriously, if that doesn't snap him out of it, you are looking at a serious addiction. You will need to assess how you feel being involved with someone with such an addiction. Chances are that if you are already feeling neglected or put off by his distasteful textual behavior, your feelings aren't likely to change. If talking about it is ineffective, encourage him to get some help, or consider moving on to someone more involved in life around them, who knows and understands that wonderful as your text life can be toward creating an amazing relationship, it is not the relationship itself!

▬▪▮▮ Repetitive Stress Injury

Now that we've talked about some of the emotional repercussions of an imbalanced text life, let's look at the physical ones. Unfortunately, too much texting can actually lead to Repetitive Stress Injury (RSI). You may have heard of Carpal Tunnel Syndrome, or Tennis Elbow, examples of RSI that occur in joints that are used repeatedly for the same action. The area around the thumb is often overworked by computer users and texters. Unless you want to suffer from slow text syndrome, in which you can no longer text quickly or painlessly, you need to take precautions to keep your fingers at their highest level of good textual health. Healthy fingers lead to good text, all around.

How do you avoid textual disorders? Fortunately, you can avoid both textual dysfunction and the pain of RSI through some of the same actions. They include the following:

- **Hands Off!** Limit the amount of time you text each day. This gives your fingers a rest and allows those around you to feel you are paying attention to them.

- **Give Your Lips a Workout:** Instead of texting all the time, increase the amount of lip action (finger-resting moments) you give; speak it rather than text it.

• Good Text Quest(ions): Stop and ask yourself, is this text even necessary? Can it wait until later? Am I being sucked into unnecessary, useless conversations? And is this really how I want to spend my time?

• Text-Free Zone: Set aside a period each day when you—gasp—turn off your cell phone. I know this can be painful, but it will strengthen your will, your fingers, and your mind! You will be creating for yourself a sacred time when nothing and no one can interrupt you. Spend the time in finger yoga, whole body relaxation, or just plain fun, free of interruption.

Chapter 10

Textual Infidelity

HE'S IN THE BATHROOM AND HIS CELL PHONE is sitting right there in front of you. Do you dare pick it up and check out his messages? A recent poll has demonstrated that thirty-three percent of men participate in textual flirtations with those other than their significant other. More disturbingly, while women are prone to view this as textual infidelity, men do not, even though it is sometimes carried over into the real world.

Before you pick up his cell, ask yourself, what am I looking for? And if I find it, what am I going to do about it? You may decide that rather than check his messages, you want to have a discussion with him about your concerns, and together define what you would consider acceptable textual behavior. It is quite possible that part of the reason for the high rate of textual flirtation is that this method of communication is still in its infancy, and you haven't looked closely enough at it to define rules and boundaries, until now.

Additionally, what one person finds acceptable may not be the same for the next. Just as you are setting boundaries for behavior toward you, you will want to make clear what you find acceptable, and what you consider a violation of trust within a serious relationship. One caveat though: If you are not in a committed relationship, whoever has texted him is none of your business, and you are probably better off not taking a peek!

◗◗◗◗ Textual Behavior

The best time to address the topic of textual infidelity is before you think it has occurred. Ask your guy his opinion on it. Ask him what level of textual intercourse (use that exact phrase, and watch his face) he would be comfortable seeing occur between you and another guy. Then ask him whether he feels either of you should be participating in textual flirtations with another.

Before you speak with your partner about this topic, think it through yourself. Get a handle on what you truly would be comfortable with. You see, we often make agreements based on what we think we can live with, without having really thought it out fully. This can lead to hurt, disappointment, and distress later on. Managing someone's expectations is an important life skill, and this is where it comes into play. If you tell someone he can expect a certain behavior to be acceptable, and then you later get upset about it and change your mind, you make him feel as though he is walking on eggshells, never really knowing what to expect.

Granted, we can't always know how we will feel in a situation. If something is genuinely intolerable for you, go ahead and say, "I thought I could handle this, but I was wrong." However, it is much better to think something through as carefully as you can before setting up an acceptable pattern of expectation; it makes for much stronger relationships overall if you can accomplish this.

Before discussing textual infidelity with your partner, sit down with yourself for a while and imagine different scenarios, and how you would feel.

Try answering some of these questions for yourself:

Do you care if he TMs with other women playfully?

Do you care if he flirt-texts with other women?

Do you care if he TMs or flirt-texts with his ex?

Do you care if he TMs a girl he knows has a crush on him?

Does the amount of TM he shares with another woman matter?
   If so, how much TM with another woman is too much?

Are these issues big enough to be deal breakers for you?

Once you know your feelings about textual fidelity, you can broach the subject with your significant other. Don't make this a challenge; bring it up at a neutral time, not when you are irritated at yet another TM from another female! In fact, it is best to have this discussion before that is an issue, if possible.

Again, ask him how he feels about textual intercourse. In fact, frame it about yourself, if you'd like, so he doesn't feel as though he's being attacked. You might say, "I've been thinking. Before you, I used to get TMs from some guys. This relationship is important to me, and I wanted to get an idea of how you feel about either of us texting others." At this point, you can leave it open to him to go first, or you can jump in and give your feelings first. Either way, make sure you each have time to speak fully and without interruption.

If you are uncomfortable with some of his answers, be honest about it. Ask yourself again how much this matters to you;

if it is serious, you must say so, unless you are ready to revisit your beliefs about it. I suggest that revisiting your beliefs about your comfort levels should be done only because someone has made a point that brings new information to light, not simply because you are afraid to lose him. If you choose your actions based on fear of losing the guy, you may well wind up losing him anyhow, because that is how resentment is born, and resentment can spiral a relationship down quickly!

One suggestion I'd make is to be sure you let him know this isn't about controlling him or his actions, but about respecting the relationship itself, if you are indeed in a monogamous relationship. As with any other conversation, approach this respectfully, speaking of your feelings and in terms of honoring one another. Finally, if his textual activity is truly intolerable for you, you may have to ask yourself whether it is a deal breaker. Remember that if someone's behavior makes you feel uncomfortable and he is unwilling to change it, it may well be time to move on. The right person *will* eventually come along, but if you're hanging on to a Mr. Right Now out of fear of being alone, you may miss Mr. Right as he walks right past you, because you seem to be involved with someone else (and are probably texting him at just that moment!).

The Serial Text-ress

There are some women who thrive on playing the temptress. Often it's just a part of their personality. They've no interest in stealing your man; they just flirt without even realizing they're doing it. If your man is spending his time sending hot messages to this textual temptress instead of you, perhaps you have cause for discussion. However, if she is merely an age-old friend, make sure their steamy exchange isn't simply the way they've always talked with each other. Sometimes making more of something than there is can actually drive others to thinking about it.

Now, hopefully you are a savvy girl and have already discussed with your partner the idea of textual fidelity, and therefore, you can quickly nip this issue in the bud. However, if you're reading this section, it may be the unfortunate case that you did not. No need to worry! Remember the goal: Focus on your intentions, right?

In this instance, I suspect your greatest intention is to disconnect the textual temptress. I would recommend you begin by talking about it with him, if you haven't already done so. This would be a great time to discuss textual fidelity. In fact, don't even initially broach it as a problem you are having with him. Instead, ask him how he feels about the idea of you having textual intercourse with others. Explain that you wouldn't want to cause him concern, but you want to get clear on this because you think it is important to be honest up front. Explain that he is really important to you and that you respect him deeply, and ask him if he feels the same about you.

You can then try explaining to him that, since you're in a committed relationship, part of what makes the relationship special is how cherished and honored he makes you feel. This can lay the groundwork for a future discussion of how when he flirts with another it makes you feel far less than cherished and adored by him. In fact, it makes you feel pretty un-special. If this is a deal breaker for him, let him know in no uncertain terms that this makes it hard for you to see the relationship as exclusive when he's carrying on in a way that you feel is emotionally betraying.

You have other options, if you don't want to end the relationship: Learn to accept it; busy up your own life, creating an ever more fabulous you, so that you enjoy life even more fully; ignore it—that may well drive him nuts; or engage in your own steamy textual intercourse with a fascinating stranger. But that only works if you can do it without feeling vindictive about it. Anger, hatred, and resentment are negative feelings that can eat away at you, so if you are experiencing any of these, it is often better to walk away from the relationship than to stay there in pain, or focused on revenge. Revenge is never good; it causes bad karma and distracts you from your true intentions.

If your intention is to create a wonderful relationship and a textual temptress is interfering in that goal, you may have to evaluate whether a guy with such weak values is the one for you.

As a last-ditch effort, you could always kindly ask her in a respectful but firm way, woman to woman, to please stop engaging with your man in this way. You may have some success with this, but it is my experience that you won't. It isn't worth getting into an argument with her; it will likely only turn nasty, and the last thing you need is to become involved in a cat fight. Bottom line: If he isn't ready to step up for you over a textual temptress, you can do far, far better!

ᴀᴧᴵᴵ Reestablishing Textual Trust

If you've been the victim of textual infidelity, trust may be hard for you in your new relationship. However, not trusting can cost you the relationship as quickly as textual infidelity can. I know, once you've felt that betrayal, it is hard to move past it, even in a new relationship. You meet some wonderful new guy, and every time his phone buzzes you feel your heart jump into your throat—is it another woman?

Textual infidelities are particularly tricky. Your typical sexual infidelity can leave you paranoid to be away from your partner, but with textual infidelity you begin to wonder whether you are safe even when he is standing right in front of you. Too, it can drive you to do some pretty crazy things if you don't watch out, such as digging through his wastebasket to glance at his phone bill, scanning through his TMs and recent calls when he goes to the restroom, and leaning your head toward him in the strangest direction in the hope of catching a glance at his incoming message.

· You may even find yourself making comments such as "Oh, Veronica again, huh?" in an unusually high-pitched voice. Well, stop it! The poor man in front of you did nothing to earn your mistrust. You cannot make him pay for those who went before him! Yes, I know it is hard to trust again. But go back to the intentions behind everything. Yes, again. I hope you sense a pattern here. Hopefully your intention with the new man in your life has to do with building a caring, trusting relationship. If that is your intention, how will your mistrust affect that?

Yes, it's hard. Guess what? You can talk with him about it, if you really feel the need to, and cannot get past it otherwise. However, I would advise you to try to get past it on your own first, especially if this is a brand-new relationship. You don't want to come off as the girl with a million neuroses! Remember, it is fine to have such feelings, but it's what you do with those feelings that matters.

So before you look at him as though he's the scum of the

earth the next time he checks his text messages, stop and take a deep breath. Tell yourself it is probably no one of importance. After all, it is *you* he is with.

I know that is easier said than done. Trust me! However, it is very important that you focus on the positives he shows you, and the ways in which he acts toward you, rather than focusing on the "what ifs." It is in the "what ifs" that we lose the gift of today, worrying about what would be otherwise. You have him here and now, right there in front of you. Focus on living in the now, on embracing the moment; that is the best way to prevent infidelity anyhow, by making each moment together precious, not by obsessing and trying to control his behavior. In fact, it is when we try to control and give in to that obsession that we are most likely to drive them away. So take a deep breath and remember that this new guy is not the old guy. This is a clean slate, and you are in a textually healthy relationship.

Chapter 11

Textual Warfare

MISCOMMUNICATION, MISUNDERSTANDING, AND misinterpretation can happen in any form of communication, but the very nature of text messaging makes it more likely to happen in this form of interaction. You and your love can be texting along happily when suddenly something goes awry. One small message is misunderstood, and soon you have an all-out textual war going on, with angry texts being spat forth faster than you can change ringtones.

What happened here? How did you go from texting sweet nothings a moment ago to throwing acid now? The truth is, you can hardly answer that yourself. It all began so innocently, and then somehow, somewhere, something was misread or mis-said, feelings were hurt, emotional tripwires triggered, and next thing you know you each feel emotionally threatened and start reacting off each other like wildfire. This kind of fighting can and does happen in relationships, for many people. However, in TM it seems escalated, as if the method of communication were a breeding ground for such trouble.

Somehow, even the most mature people can find themselves sucked into the textual battlefield. There seems to be something almost imperceptibly seductive about the small, taunting TM that just begs to be answered. Yes, you know you should just delete the angry message you just received. In fact, you know you shouldn't read the next seven that pop into your inbox like exploding bullets, but you can't help yourself—you do it. And, in the same way, you know you shouldn't respond, but the bullets keep flying, and the need to defend yourself seems to rise up and take hold, and even though you know you shouldn't, even though it somehow feels like a ridiculous high school mind-game, you find yourself engaged in full-on textual warfare.

Textual Misunderstanding

If you proceed to carry out the ensuing debate in text messages when already operating on a misunderstanding, it is likely only going to get worse. Rather than sending back an angry retort, why not take a deep breath, count to ten, and then either call and speak to your text partner on the phone, or text back that you think you need to clear your head right now and would like to talk about it in person this evening.

To continue discussing the misunderstanding in a medium that is so restrictive (only 160 characters, come on!), and devoid of important factors such as tonality and voice inflection, is usually a mistake and likely to lead to greater hurt feelings that come with the territory when we feel we are being attacked, and in need of defending ourselves. I know you may feel driven to send additional texts in an effort to bring clarity, and while on some occasions this can help, a lot of times it does not. If you want to try a few simple texts to shed some light on the situation, go for it, but if you see the issue escalating, it is time to disengage and address it in person, where you can express yourself more clearly, and have the added benefit of body language, tonality, and so forth. It is likely that the absence of one of those factors has contributed to the misunderstanding in the first place, so it is usually best to move the disagreement into an arena that can at least bring those elements back into play.

So what are your action steps when a battle breaks out? If it cannot be quickly cleared up (in about three texts or less), politely disengage and handle the rest on the phone or in person. When you do get together to speak, try to keep in mind that this is someone you care for deeply, and that it isn't likely so much an instance of "who is right or wrong" as much as one of "let's see where we got off track and misunderstood each other." Why would you do this? Because it is probably true; it's true in a majority of disagreements, and in TM it is far more likely.

TM can be an amazing gift that can keep you connected and improve your communication, but the brevity of the message, the lack of emotion, or tone, and the rapid-fire pace with which most people shoot off a text, can pack a serious punch. This is especially true of communication with someone we are romantically involved with, as we girls tend to read so much more into things of that nature to begin with.

An important thing to note here: If you are doing as I suggested throughout this book, focusing on your intention for the interaction, it is *really* hard to engage in a full-out text war. Why? Because with each new message you ask yourself what your intent is for the message. When dealing with someone you like or love, this will likely bring you back, and you will recall that your goals for interaction are to help your relationship grow, not to tear each other down. That simple little question can cause you to pause before sending a potentially damaging TM.

What most people don't seem to internalize is that the cold things we say when angry never totally go away. They become part of the subconscious, embedded in our psyche. For this and many other reasons, we should try to refrain from saying cold or hurtful things that can degrade the relationship on many levels for a long time to come. Asking yourself your intent before hitting the *send* button can help you keep your textual life, even when in disagreement, in greater integrity. Don't underestimate the power of this question, or the effect a text war can have on your relationship. For your sake, and the sake of your relationship, I hope you fight clean. If you keep the focus on the intention, that will be a lot easier to do.

What's your three-step action plan if you find yourself embroiled in textual warfare?

Textual Engagement

As with other forms of communication, addressing textual warfare before it happens is the best way to avoid this plague. Talking with your partner about the possibility that you could at some time wind up in a miscommunication, and determining in advance how you will handle it, can go a long way toward keeping you out of a textual battle.

I'm sure you can see the wisdom of structuring your world to minimize disagreement. Creating rules with which to handle it not only will help determine the outcome, but will also demonstrate that you consider the relationship important enough to take the time to develop them in the first place.

Perhaps developing rules of textual engagement for times of strife may seem counterintuitive: You don't want to imagine ever fighting with the one you love! However, the reality is that people disagree, and that especially with TM you have a lot of room for misinterpretation and misunderstanding. If you set up rules for engagement during a neutral time, when you are both happy and feeling quite loving toward each other, it can go a long way in helping prevent all-out textual warfare, and in supporting and nurturing your relationship.

What kind of rules would you make? It depends on your relationship, of course. If you know there are certain topics that cause a lot of strife between you two, you may want to keep those topics out of the TM arena. However, there are also a lot of rules that would apply to most people, like how you will handle the disagreement. Will you want to put a cap on the number of argumentative messages that can pass between you before talking about it in person instead? Or how about "no unfair texting/attacks when the other party can't respond, such as when they are at work"?

Other rules may apply to how you talk with each other in text, rules that remind you always to treat each other respectfully, even in the midst of an argument, and even in something as trivial as a TM.

What rules of engagement would make sense for you during times of disagreement?

Reducing Textual Tension

If your text partner seems to have misunderstood you, and you're not in a position to call or speak with him, state in your text that you think you have been misunderstood. Try one more time to clarify, and if he still doesn't seem to understand, explain that it must be you aren't communicating the way you had hoped to and that you'd like to discuss it later in the evening. If he proceeds to "push" you, refuse to engage in an all-out text war. Explain that you honor and care for him enough to recognize this as too important to relegate to text messages where there can be too many possible misunderstandings, and hold your ground.

⬛▪️📶 Textual Humiliation

Remember that even though you're angry right now, this is the guy you are in, or may in the future want to be in, a serious relationship with. Isn't part of liking/loving someone wanting to help him be at his best when moving through the world? Wouldn't you want your partner to think that way about you? Is it not a conflicting message to tell someone you like/love him, and want to see him happy, and then put him into a publicly embarrassing position? Do you think this is perhaps unfair? What credibility does it lend to your words? Too few women consider this when they release an angry burst of emotion. Do your actions match your words?

The way we behave when in an argument can tell a lot about us. Let's be honest; it is easy to behave kindly and lovingly when life is good. It is who we are in the difficult moments that can really show our true colors.

Your goal: Go back to your intention in the bigger scheme of things, which is always to honor and respect those who are important to you. Yes indeed, sometimes they can make that *really* challenging. However, if you are honest in your goal to love, then you must do your best always to uphold that good behavior, even when you are angry or frustrated.

Do your best to avoid textual humiliation. Go back over the rules for *Good Clean Text*, always keep your intentions in the forefront of your mind, and do your best to treat your partner as you want to be treated, especially during times of strife. Do this and you will be a huge step closer to living the relationship of your dreams, and honoring your partner in the process. Use your textual powers for good!

Chapter 12

Wide World of Textual Relations

NOW THAT YOU'RE AN EXPERT ON TEXTUAL communication, it's time to enjoy a healthy text life. If, however, you've come this far only to find yourself without a text partner, well, you have a wide new world of possibilities before you.

In this day and age there arise daily new methods for meeting the possible love of your life, and many of these new-fangled relationships are text-based ones. You can find a potential mate through text-based dating services, text dating parties, and online text discussion groups. These interesting new options will allow you to break the ice in ways never before experienced, and even to watch out for potential partners as they appear on your radar, giving you the opportunity to reach out with some good vibrations before they move out of your range forever. Let's take a look at some of the new methods for dating and relating with potential new loves in the cellular age.

▂▄█ Text Parties

Imagine entering a bar, looking around, and seeing a guy you would love to talk to, but you're just too shy. Well, why not look at the number on his shirt and send him a text from across the room? This is an option at one of the many text dating parties springing up around the globe.

At these "silent parties" members text one another messages across the room, breaking the ice in a way that feels less emotionally dangerous than confronting possible rejection face-to-face. Popular among business professionals in their twenties and thirties, this new trend in dating seems to be springing up on both sides of the pond, with roots in England, yet quickly spreading to the U.S.

Typical attendees are often too busy to find potential relationships through traditional methods, and appreciate the convenience and safety of approaching a potential date in this manner. Additionally, they often feel braver about disclosing information in writing than they may verbally.

If you think about it, maybe this makes sense. The Internet had a profound effect upon the ways in which people met and dated, ranging from introductions through chat rooms, online gaming and forums, to official dating sites such as Match.com and eharmony.com. It makes sense that technology such as the cell phone would be the follow-up to that approach. Plus, text dating parties have the advantage of your being able to see people right in front of your eyes, to sense if there is some chemistry there, before you invest too much time in getting to know them.

On the downside, others are getting your number, which gives them easy access to you. Some parties have found ways around this, by having you text a third party which then forwards it on. I would recommend you seek one of those parties, rather than an arrangement where your number is made publicly known, for safety reasons, if no other.

I will admit, it sounded weird to me at first, even a bit creepy. But as some who have experimented with this new dating scene have found, it really isn't much different from going to a bar or nightclub—except that instead of having guys hitting on you over cocktails, they TM you. That makes it a lot *less* creepy, not to mention easier to reject them if you're not interested. Somehow, just ignoring their text or typing "no thanks" feels better than having to let them down to their face. Though I suppose for a guy it isn't so great; otherwise you might have given him a shot out of pity, or your inability to turn him down. Another plus is that it's fun to see guys have to step up to the challenge. They need to be creative to make their TM stand out from the others, so you get to see who is more clever right up front. That teaches you something about his approach to challenges, not to mention his sense of humor, and even intellect, to some degree.

As you can see, there are pros and cons. It may be for you, or then again, it may not. Either way, the world of text dating is beginning to grow in popularity and will probably be around for a while. One piece of advice, though: Remember your safety when meeting a stranger through this or any method.

Text Services

You've tried eharmony and ematch, you've trolled chat rooms, and still, you just haven't found Mr. Right. Maybe you, like many, have grown impatient with the whole dating process. Why not try a new level of dating? It is almost like micro-dating. With text message dating services you can determine in a few short textual contacts whether you want to continue getting to know this potential textual partner.

These services are pretty fascinating. Each works a bit differently, but the basics go like this: You sign up and create a profile. Then when you go out and about, you text your location to the service and it will search to see if there is anyone in your vicinity whose profile is a good fit for yours. If so, they will text you the profile and you can begin corresponding, then meet face-to-face, if you so choose.

These services are gaining popularity around the globe, but they are especially groundbreaking in India, where arranged marriages have been the norm, and where premarital dating has been limited they are having a tremendous impact on the social structure there, opening new doors for men and women alike. In a nation such as that, text dating not only transforms the dating scene, but actually can influence the social order, which makes this new technology pretty powerful.

▃▃▊▊ Text Forums

You can get together for both fun and pleasure at a text forum online, where you can download ringtones, exchange text message ideas, and encode or decode text messages. These are websites that allow you to utilize your phone and TM more fully, as they help you maximize your understanding of different features, and introduce you to many other ways to use the myriad features on the cell phones of today.

You can find TM dictionaries, encode or decode messages, find speed-building exercises so you can text more quickly, and, of course, enjoy lots of social networking with other TM users, whom you can talk with both at the forums and, if you click, through TM too. These sites are also great places to find awesome examples of TMs of every kind: funny, romantic, breakup, makeup—you name it, you can find it! So if you want to maximize your textual experience, check out one of these sites.

Please feel free to visit mine at www.TheArtOfText.com.

As I hope you have come to realize, there are numerous potentials in the world of TM. The trick is using your texting for good so that it enhances, not unhinges your relationships. Fully embracing your textuality with conscious intent can lead to a beautiful relationship that honors both you and that special guy in your life. With something as simple as your sleek little cell phone, you can wield tremendous power in shaping and molding your romance, setting boundaries, and creating expectations and standards for excellent behavior. You can manage your time and emotions in such a way as to create a relationship of the highest order, all while fingering stimulating messages designed to add textual excitement to your day, one little text at a time!

The power is not in the TM, but in the user behind it. Master the methods you learned in this book and apply them with the focus of intent at all times, and you'll be not only textually fulfilled, but fully in control of your text life. Use it poorly and without thought to the intent, and you take a dire risk with a powerful communication device. You own the power to define how TM will affect your life. Fill it with good vibrations and wield that cell phone wisely!

Emoticon Dictionary

EMOTICON	MEANING
:) :-) :] :-]	You're smiling or joking, or are feeling happy.
;) ;-)	You're winking.
:-||	You're upset.
>:(	You're very angry.
:(:-(:[:-[:-<	You're sad.
:'-(	You're crying.
:/ :-Q	You're not sure or you're confused.
;-^)	You're being tongue-in-cheek.
:-}	You're embarrassed.
>:D	You're showing malicious joy.
:-*	You're giving a kiss.
:-P	You're sticking your tongue out.
=)	Wow!

Text Abbreviation Dictionary

ABBREVIATION	MEANING
^5	High Five
2Nite	Tonight
AKA	Also Known As
B/C	Because
B4	Before
BB	Be Back
BBL	Be Back Later
BCNU	Be Seein' You
BF	Boyfriend
BFF	Best Friends Forever
BRB	Be Right Back
BTDT	Been There, Done That
BTW	By the Way
BZ	Busy
UCMU	You Crack Me Up

COS	Change of Subject
CSL	Can't Stop Laughing
C-T	City
CUL8R	See You Later
EZ	Easy
G1	Good One
G2G	Got to Go
GF	Girlfriend
Gratz	Congratulations
H&K	Hugs and Kisses
H/O	Hold On
HV	Have
IK	I Know
ILU	I Love You
IMU	I Miss You
JIC	Just in Case
JK	Just Kidding
JP	Just Playing
L8R	Later
LOL	Laugh Out Loud

MSG	Message
NBD	No Big Deal
NE1	Anyone
NM	Not Much
NOYB	None of Your Business
NSA	No Strings Attached
NVM	Nevermind
OIC	Oh I See
OMG	Oh My God
ORLY	Oh Really?
OTB	Off to Bed
Peeps	People
PLZ	Please
PPL	People
Prolly	Probably
PZ	Peace
RLY	Really
RME	Rolling My Eyes
RUOK?	Are You Okay?
SBT	Sorry About That

STFU	Shut the "Freak" Up
Str8	Straight
TBH	To Be Honest
TC	Take Care
TTYL	Talk to You Later
TY	Thank You
U	You
U2	You Too
UR	Your; You're
W/B	Write Back
W/E	Whatever
WAN2TLK	Want to Talk
WC	Who Cares
WK	Week
WTG	Way to Go
WU	What's Up?
Y	Why?
YT?	You There?
YW	You're Welcome
ZZZ	Tired or Bored

Acknowledgments

My deepest gratitude to the following people:

To Jordana Tusman at Running Press, an angel of an editor,
for her outstanding help in shaping this book.

To the team at Running Press, for their fantastic work at every
turn of this project. A big thank-you to Amanda Richmond for
her thoughtful book design and to Wendi Koontz for all the
fabulous illustrations. Many thanks to the publicity team for all
their hard work. And deep appreciation to Jon Anderson.

To Jackie Meyer, my agent, for her support throughout
this process.

To Alyssa Kramer, my assistant, for her excellent research,
and her cheerful commitment and support.

To Rob Bach, Mark Melaccio, and NKC, who helped me to
better understand the importance of text within the context
of relationships.

To Danielle Simonian, for her love, support, and constant

encouragement at every turn of the road, as well as important lessons on the spaces and places for TM in our lives.

To Brandon and Chris, for their love, patience, and encouragement.

To James Bach, my life partner, with whom I share a love that was built upon a highly textual foundation.

And finally, to all those who have had the courage to go deep with me—to have loved, to have shared, to have risen up—and who have had the courage to tell their story.